# THE US 8th Air Force

# IN CAMERA

## 1942–1944

Anthony Ralph Carcione, a Thunderbolt pilot in the 62nd Fighter Squadron, 56th Fighter Group, his mom, Elizabeth, and friend, Byron Morrill, during leave, Christmas 1943. Carcione, who was born on 26 January 1919, was one of the first permanent pilots out of flight school to arrive at Bradley US Army Air Field, Windsor Locks, Connecticut, in the summer of 1942. During a training mission out of Bradley he made what appeared to be a forced landing at A.B.E. airport near his home town in Pennsylvania. A week later, a newspaper arrived at Bradley Field sporting a photo of Tony's 'forced landing' with the headline reading, 'Local Boy Drops In To See Family!' Hubert Zemke, his CO, disciplined Tony by grounding him for a month and made him Group Photo Officer. One of his photos, of Colonel Dave Schilling's dog, Buddy, was sent to Walt Disney Studios and became Disney's model for the 62nd 'Fighting Bulldogs' logo used on the squadron's flight jackets. In England, Carcione flew P-47 42-7937 *Triss*, then 47-275855 *Tony*. His visit home at Christmas 1943 was the last time his mother saw her son. Carcione was killed in action on 8 March 1943, when he was shot down flying 42-74697 over Belgium. His body was brought back home to the USA in 1949 and laid to rest with a military funeral in Wind Gap, Pennsylvania. His parents, Basil and Elizabeth, took their grief to their graves.

56th FG WWII Association via Alan Hague

# THE US 8th Air Force
# IN CAMERA

## PEARL HARBOR to D-DAY

### 1942–1944

MARTIN W. BOWMAN

SUTTON PUBLISHING LIMITED

First published in 1997 by
Sutton Publishing Limited · Phoenix Mill
·Thrupp · Stroud · Gloucestershire · GL5 2BU

British Library Cataloguing in Publication Data
A catalogue record for this book is available from the British Library

ISBN 0 7509 1680 X

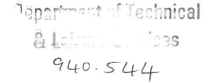
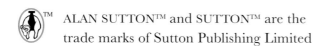
™ ALAN SUTTON™ and SUTTON™ are the
trade marks of Sutton Publishing Limited

Typeset in 11/15 pt Baskerville.
Typesetting and origination by
Sutton Publishing Limited.
Printed in Great Britain by
Butler & Tanner, Frome, Somerset.

# INTRODUCTION

Volume One of *The US 8th Air Force In Camera* covers its activation in England in 1942, from its humble beginnings with just a handful of heavy bomb groups and fighter units, to the massive armada poised to support the D-Day landings in June 1944. While the book is not intended to provide a day-to-day, in-depth photographic history, a cross-section of the many thousands of contemporary images is presented to give an overall picture of almost every feature of bomber and fighter, air and ground activities, operational duty and leisure moments. Even some of their adversaries in the Luftwaffe are included.

Many of the photos are published here for the first time. Those that have been seen before are included because they illustrate a particular facet, or because they contain additional information or new data not presented before. Many of the images were shot by combat photographers and the crews themselves. Combat cameramen faced exactly the same hazards and enemy action as the crews. During the filming of the morale-boosting documentary *Memphis Belle* in 1943, for instance, Lieutenant Harold Tannenbaum and four other combat photographers were lost on board

Fortresses which failed to return from raids over enemy-occupied territory.

A whole host of evocative and atmospheric pictures have also been kindly forwarded from the private collections of many individuals in several countries, to help re-create this uniquely nostalgic period in Anglo-American aviation folklore. All of these photographs provide a revealing and fascinating insight into the world's greatest air force in history. At peak personnel strength, the 8th Air Force numbered more than 200,000 officers and enlisted men. The USAAF originally had 75 airfields in the UK, but the total finally reached 250. At peak operating strength, it numbered 40½ heavy bomb groups, 15 fighter groups and 2 photo-reconnaissance groups operating from bases in the UK. At this strength, a typical mission consisted of 1,400 heavy bombers, escorted by 800 fighters.

Famous aircraft, such as *Memphis Belle*, *Suzy Q*, *Witchcraft*, and *Yankee Doodle Dandy*, to name but a few, are covered, along with their crews, as the 8th begins missions over occupied Europe, from the early daylight raids by B-24 Liberators and B-17 Flying Fortresses on the French coastal ports and U-boat pens on the Brittany coast, to the deeper penetration raids, into France and later Germany, against marshalling yards, steelworks, power stations and tank factories. On 27 January 1943, to demonstrate that daylight precision bombing could triumph over area bombing by night, General Ira C. Eaker sent 91 B-17s and B-24s on the first American raid on Germany, when the U-boat construction yards at Wilhelmshaven were attacked. Bad weather reduced the attacking force to 53 B-17s, which dropped their bombs on the shipyards from 25,000 ft through a German smoke screen, while two others bombed Emden. Despite heavy fighter opposition only three bombers were lost.

In June 1943 Operation POINTBLANK, an intermediate priority objective aimed at the German fighter strength, was finally published. Primary objectives listed were the U-boat yards and bases, the remainder of the German aircraft industry, ball-bearings and oil, while the secondary objectives were synthetic rubber and tyres and military motor transport vehicles. (On 22 June the first really deep penetration of Germany took place when 235 B-17s bombed the synthetic rubber plant at Huls.) The objective concluded that the reduction of the German fighter force was of primary importance, and that any delay in its prosecution would make the task 'progressively more difficult'. The plan called for 2,702 heavy bombers in fifty-one groups to be in place before the Allied invasion, scheduled for mid-1944.

During June 1943 the 94th, 95th and 96th Bomb Groups formed a new 4th Bomb Wing in Essex and Suffolk under the command of Brigadier-General Fred L. Anderson. Following high losses, the 8th Air Force B-26 groups were transferred from the 3rd Bomb Wing to 8th Air Support Command for future medium-level bombing operations in a tactical role. This move was intended to give the Marauders longer-range fighter cover. Their Essex bases were taken over by three Fortress groups in the 4th Wing, commanded by Colonel Curtis E. LeMay, while the arrival of the 100th, 385th and 388th Bomb Groups increased the 4th Wing to six groups. By September 1943 8th Bomber Command possessed nine groups of the 1st Bomb Wing and four B-24 groups of the 2nd.

On 17 July 1943 a record 322 8th Air Force bombers were despatched, to Hanover, and then, on 24 July, Blitz Week began with an attack by 324 B-17s from the 1st and 4th Wings on targets in Norway, with one force flying a 2,000 mile round trip to Bergen and Trondheim; the longest American mission over Europe so far. Some 167 bombers from the 1st Wing bombed Heroya and completely devastated a factory complex, while 41 bombers bombed shipping at Trondheim. Blitz Week cost the 8th Air Force approximately 100 aircraft and 90 combat crews, leaving fewer than 200 heavies for combat.

Further afield, missions were flown from North Africa when the three Liberator groups in England – the 44th, 93rd, and 389th – joined with Liberators in the 98th and 376th Bomb Groups of the 9th Air Force in Libya, and on 1 August 1943 a total of 177 B-24Ds bombed the Ploesti oilfields in Romania from low level in Operation TIDAL WAVE. Malfunctions and accidents en route reduced the effectiveness of the force, and navigational errors caused severe problems in the target area, forcing some groups to bomb one another's assigned targets. Delayed-action bombs from preceding groups damaged or destroyed B-24s in the following groups. Some 167 Liberators actually attacked their targets and dropped 311 tons of bombs on the refineries, but 54 B-24Ds were lost over the targets and 3 more crashed at sea. Seven crews were interned in Turkey, while 19 landed in Cyprus, Sicily or Malta. Of the 92 which returned to North Africa, 55 had suffered varying degrees of battle damage. Forty-two per cent of the plants' refining capacity and 40 per cent of its cracking capacity were destroyed, but most of the refineries were repaired and within a month were operating at pre-mission capacity again. All five groups received Presidential Unit Citations, while five Medals of Honor were awarded (three posthumously). At the end of August, after more raids from Benghazi, the three 8th Air Force groups were ordered back to England.

In England meanwhile, on 17 August, the Fortress groups of the 1st and 3rd Bomb Divisions carried out a daring double strike on Regensburg and Schweinfurt. Some 376 Fortresses bombed the Schweinfurt ball-bearing plant and the aircraft plants at Regensburg, which were estimated to produce 200 Bf 109s a month, about 25–30 per cent of Germany's single-engine aircraft production. Some 60 B-17s were shot down (36 from the 1st Wing at Schweinfurt and 24 from the 4th Wing at Regensburg), while 27 B-17s were so badly damaged that they never flew again. Another 60 B-17s of the 4th Wing, which continued to North Africa after bombing the target, had to be left behind in North Africa for repair.

The heavy losses were repeated when the Forts went back to the ball-bearing factories at Schweinfurt on 14 October. Some 291 B-17s attacked, but 60 Fortresses were lost, and damage was sustained to 138 B-17s that returned to England. These losses marked the urgent need for a long-range fighter to escort the bombers to and from their targets, and led to the long overdue introduction of the P-51 Mustang, although P-38 Lightnings and P-47 Thunderbolts carried out most of the escort duty throughout the rest of 1943.

The week 20–26 February saw a series of fierce actions which came to be known as 'Big Week', when the full might of the 8th Air Force was turned on the enemy's aircraft industry in a concentrated period for the first time. Total losses, though, amounted to 226 bombers. Then, in March 1944, the 8th started its assault on 'Big B' – Berlin. On 4 March thirty-one B-17s bombed the Kleinmachnow area south-west of Berlin, to become the first US bombers to attack the Reich capital. Two days later, 730 heavy bombers and almost 800 escort fighters were despatched to 'Big B' again. April and May followed with a mix of strategic bombing raids on oil and other industrial targets, and tactical targets in France, for the build-up to the invasion of Europe. By June the interdiction campaign to isolate north-western France, the area of Operation OVERLORD, was in full swing.

# ACKNOWLEDGEMENTS

I am most grateful to the following individuals and organizations throughout England, the USA and the Continent, who have dug deep into their photographic collections and archives to unearth many 'gems', some of which have never before been published: Steve Adams; Christine Armes; Boeing Aircraft Co.; Mike Bailey; Cliff Bishop; Stan Bishop; Dr Theo Boiten; Charles L. Brown; Colonel William B. Cameron USAF (Ret'd); Hugh K. Crawford Collection; Abe Dolim; William Donald; Douglas Aircraft Co.; Pat Everson; Robert Foose; Larry Goldstein; Alan Hague; the late Cliff Hatcher; the late Urzal P. Harvel; the late Russ D. Hayes; the late Alan Healy; Andy Height; the late Howard Hernan; Herman Hetzel; Colonel Dexter Hodge USAF (Ret'd); Mick Jennings; Jim Kidder; Jim Kotapish; Richard H. Lewis; Lockheed Aircraft; Ian McLachlan; Hugh R. McLaren; Coots Matthews; Gus Mencow; John A. Miller; Eric Mombeek; Colonel William Odell; Merle Olmstead; John Page; Cliff Pyle; Pat Ramm; Connie and Gordon Richards; the late Bill Robertie; Paul Tibbets; Elmer Reinhart; Francis X. Sheehan; Hans-Heiri Stapfer; Frank Thomas; Thorpe Abbotts Memorial Museum; Steve Snelling; Geoff Ward; Gordon B. Wheeler; Truett Woodall; Sam Young.

# THE
# US 8TH AIR FORCE
# IN CAMERA

## 1942–1944

America – the 'arsenal of democracy'. Long before the USA's entry into the Second World War, President Roosevelt helped Britain by way of the Lend-Lease Act. After the Japanese attack on Pearl Harbor, 7 December 1941, the country stepped up its war production and companies such as Douglas at Long Beach, and Lockheed Vega, Burbank, California, supplemented Boeing Aircraft, Seattle, Washington, in producing B-17 Flying Fortresses. These are B-17F-DL models on the Douglas production line.

Douglas

A total of 18,188 B-24 Liberators were turned out by five factories in America during the Second World War. Production began at the Consolidated plant in San Diego, California. During 1942 a second Liberator production line was opened at Fort Worth, Texas, by Convair, while a third production line was brought into operation at Douglas, Tulsa, Oklahoma. At the end of 1942 a fourth B-24 production line was opened, by the Ford Motor Company, at Willow Run, Dearborn, Michigan. Early in 1943 the fifth and final major Liberator plant was operated by North American at Dallas, Texas.

Douglas

Young men came from every state in the Union to join up after Pearl Harbor, and of course many thousands enlisted in the USAAF and the 8th Air Force bound for Great Britain. These aviation cadets assigned for primary flying training at Darr Aero Tech, Albany, Georgia, receive their flying instructions from a pretty young dispatcher.

Gordon B. Wheeler Collection

Aviation cadets, all of whom started at Lincoln, Nebraska, went through Basic at Twenty-Nine Palms, California, 200 miles east of Los Angeles, late in 1943. Left to right: Robert L. Miller, Aberdeen, Washington; Jack B. Nichols, Wilcox, Arizona; Arthur L. Pekarek, Long Beach, California; Robert J. Walker, Portland, Oregon; Seymour Thurber, Sonoita, Arizona; Loon R. Milner, Provo, Utah. Miller flew missions as a B-17 pilot in the 493rd Bomb Group at Debach, England, while Milner was shot down flying a B-17 on his first mission.

Robert L. Miller via Truett Woodall

After primary training, those aviation cadets who gained their 'wings' progressed onto basic and flew the AT-6 Texan Basic Trainer which was derived from the earlier BT-9 trainer, one of which is seen here before the war over Randolph Field, Texas. The BT-9 (NA-16), which was powered by a 400 hp Wright Whirlwind engine and had a fixed, spatted main undercarriage, first flew in April 1936. The BT-9 was succeeded by the improved BT-14 version ordered in 1940. The AT-6 Texan, or Harvard, derived from the NA-26, an NA-16 variant which in March 1937 won an Air Corps design competition for a 'basic combat' trainer. Some forty-one BC-1 trainers, powered by 600 hp Pratt & Whitney engines, were followed by the world famous AT-6 (the BC designation changed to AT-6A in 1940) and this became the standard trainer used by the AAC and other air arms in the Second World War. Some 912 AT-6As were built and were followed by 2,970 AT-6C models and a further 4,388 AT-6D models.

Gordon B. Wheeler Collection

'Me and my friends'. Herman Hetzel, who became a cameraman in the 457th Bomb Squadron, 303rd Bomb Group, a B-17 outfit, poses on a donkey at Alamogordo training field, New Mexico, in the summer of 1942. Hetzel was later to join the 458th Bomb Group, a Liberator unit in the Second Bombardment Division, 8th Air Force.

Herman Hetzel via Christine Armes

B-24D Liberators on the line in Nevada during phase training. All air echelons in the heavy bombardment groups trained at air bases such as this, prior to going overseas to the theatres of war, where they were reunited with their ground echelon, usually at the base in the European Theatre of Operations. '080', the nearest Liberator, is *Sgt Stepanski*.

Herman Hetzel via Christine Armes

Boeing B-17E Flying Fortress in flight over New Mexico. Like the B-24 groups, B-17 units completed their phase training at remote bases such as Alamogordo, and at others across the vast USA, from Sarasota, Florida, to Walla Walla, Washington, and Pocatello, Idaho, to Muroc Lake Air Base, California.

Herman Hetzel via Christine Armes

Prior to overseas movement there was little time or opportunity to indulge in leisure pursuits or visit the nearest town, if there was one, so these airmen, billeted in tents at a remote desert air base, pass an evening playing cards.

Herman Hetzel via Christine Armes

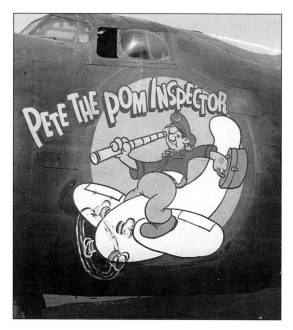

Groups were only deemed ready for overseas service once the POM (Preparation for Overseas Movement) inspectors were satisfied. Consolidated B-24D-53-CO 42-40370 *Pete the POM Inspector* became famous in the 467th Bomb Group at Rackheath, Norfolk.

The late Alan Healy

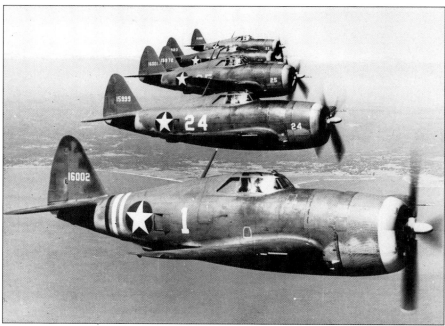

One of the first fighter groups earmarked for the 8th Air Force in England was the 56th, which had been activated at Savannah, Georgia (where the 8th Air Force was activated, on 28 January 1942), as far back as 15 January 1941. In December 1942 the 56th Fighter Group was alerted for overseas movement. This section of six P-47Bs in formation during an air defence patrol sortie high over the Atlantic seaboard in 1942 belongs to the 61st Fighter Squadron and is led by Colonel Hub Zemke in 41-6002 '1'.

USAF via Mike Bailey

On 2 January 1942 the order activating the 8th Air Force had been signed by Major-General Henry Arnold, the Commanding General, AAF. On 22 February VIIIth Bomber Command was formally activated at High Wycombe, Buckinghamshire, under the command of Brigadier-General Ira C. Eaker.

USAF

Captain Bill Odell (right) and his gunner, Sergeant Earl Thompson, discuss the 4 July mission with senior officers after returning from the raid on Haamstaede airfield which was led by Flight-Lieutenant A.B. Wheeler, RAF. Hits were achieved on administration buildings, a hangar and dispersal points. After the bombing Odell zigged and zagged while 8 miles out, and then closed up waiting for fighters. None came. He reached the coast and was the first one home. On 8 November the 15th Light Bombardment Squadron was transferred from the 8th Air Force to the 12th Air Force, moving to North Africa to take part in Operation TORCH on 15 November. Based at Youks le Bain, Tabessa, Algeria, the squadron arrived five days after the invasion and was operational within a week. The 15th was later absorbed into the 47th Bomb Group in Africa and inactivated.

USAF

The first 8th Air Force involvement in a mission to drop bombs on an enemy target was on 4 July 1942 – Independence Day – when six of the twelve A-20 Bostons belonging to 226 Squadron RAF at Swanton Morley, a grass airfield in Norfolk, carried American crews of the 15th Bomb Squadron (Light) in attacks on four airfields in Holland. The senior ranking US officer was Captain Charles Kegelman (seen here second from left beside '*Keg*'), who attacked De Kooy airfield in AL750 'Z', crewed by Lieutenant R.M. Dorton, navigator, Sergeant Bennie Cunningham, rear gunner, and Technical Sergeant R.L. Goley, dorsal gunner. Kegelman's starboard engine took a direct hit and burst into flames, and the propeller flew off. The right wing tip struck the ground, and the fuselage actually bounced on the surface of De Kooy aerodrome, tearing a hole in the belly of the bomber. Lifting the Boston back into the air on one engine, Kegelman headed for the Channel. A flak tower on Den Helder airfield opened up, and the young captain returned fire with his nose guns. He lifted the Boston over the tower and headed for England with the right engine on fire. The fire went out over the Channel, and Kegelman continued home to Swanton Morley, hugging the waves across the North Sea. Charles Kegelman rose rapidly in promotion. From April to 8 November 1943 he was a lieutenant-colonel in command of the 48th Fighter Group at William Northern Field, Tennessee. On 12 November he assumed command of the 337th Fighter Group at Sarasota, Florida, as a full colonel. On 16 November 1944 he assumed command of the 42nd Bomb Group at Sansapor, New Guinea, which by March 1945 was operating North American B-25 Mitchells from Moratai. On 10 March Kegelman's aircraft was involved in a mid-air collision with his wingman and he was killed. Kegelman airfield, near Cherokee, Oklahoma, is named in his memory.

USAF

The most successful attack by the twelve Bostons on 4 July 1942 was the attack on Bergen Alkmaar by three aircraft led by Flight-Lieutenant 'Yogi' Yates Earl, RAF. In this photograph the bomb bursts can be seen (bottom right). Of the four airfield targets, Bergen Alkmaar was the only one which was attacked successfully. Two American crews were lost on the raids. Lieutenant Jack Loehrl was hit by flak north of De Kooy airfield, and he and his two gunners, Sergeants Wright and Whitham, were killed, while Lieutenant Marshall Draper, the bombardier, survived and became the first American airman to be taken prisoner. AL741 'V', flown by Lieutenant Stan G. Lynn, was hit by flak after bombing Bergen Alkmaar, and crashed on the airfield, killing all on board.

USAF

B-17E 41-9129 had a troubled crossing to England after leaving Presque Isle for Goose Bay on 22 June 1942, but finally arrived at Prestwick in Scotland on 24 July 1942 after repairs to mend a broken tail wheel sustained in an accident at Bathurst, New Brunswick. This Fortress was assigned to the 359th Bomb Squadron, 303rd Bomb Group, forming the BOLERO weather flight, and went on to serve the 97th, 92nd and 305th Bomb Groups before leaving the 1st Wing in 1943.

USAF via Mike Bailey

The first Fortress group to become operational in England in 1942 was the 97th Bomb Group, which operated from Polebrook, and Grafton Underwood, Northamptonshire, equipped with the B-17E. 41-9023 *Yankee Doodle* of the 414th Bomb Squadron was one of twelve Fortresses that took part in the first B-17 mission of the war, on 17 August 1942, and carried Brigadier-General Ira C. Eaker to Rouen. Note the RAF-style camouflage. This aircraft later served with the 92nd and 91st Bomb Groups.

USAF

Crew of B-17F-10-BO 41-24444 *The Red Gremlin* (renamed *Superman* when it was assigned to the 92nd Bomb Group, on 24 August), in the 340th Bomb Squadron, 97th Bomb Group, 9 September 1942. Back row, left to right: Major Paul W. Tibbets, Ryan, Tom Ferebee, 'Dutch' Van Kirk, Hughes and Splitt. Front row: Peach, Quate, Fitzgerald, Gowan and Fittsworth. On 17 August 1942 Tibbets elected to use 41-2578 *Butcher Shop* and Lieutenant Butcher's crew to lead the first Fortress raid of the war with his CO, Colonel Frank A. Armstrong Jr. Tibbets, his bombardier, Tom Ferebee, and navigator, 'Dutch' Van Kirk, flew the same positions in *Enola Gay* on the first atomic bomb drop, on Hiroshima, Japan, 6 August 1945.

Paul Tibbets Collection

Lend-Lease in reverse. Britain reciprocated with the supply of badly needed aircraft and facilities when the Americans were initially found wanting. One of the aircraft supplied to the embryonic 8th Air Force was the superlative Supermarine Spitfire, various marks of which the USAAF used in the fighter and photo-reconnaissance roles, equipping the 4th, 31st, 52nd, and 350th Fighter Groups, the 67th Reconnaissance Group, and the 7th Photo Group.

Richards Collection

B-24 Liberators of the 93rd Bomb Group for as far as the eye can see, pictured in North Africa late in September 1942 while en route to England via South America and the South Atlantic, to join the First Bombardment Wing, 8th Bomber Command, at Alconbury, Cambridgeshire. 'Ted's Travelling Circus' (so named after its CO, Colonel Ted Timberlake, and its many sojourns in North Africa during 1942–3), flew its first mission on 9 October 1942.

USAF

An American Red Cross Clubmobile (a converted British bus) serves refreshments to ground crews of the 92nd Bomb Group working on B-17E *Phyllis*, 41-9020 at Bovingdon, from where it made several courier flights to North Africa late in 1942. Clubmobiles were first introduced in 1942 and were manned by Red Cross girls who dispensed cups of hot coffee, cigarettes, chewing gum, doughnuts and newspapers free of charge. By the end of 1943, there were fifty in operation, each servicing detachments six miles or more from a club. Bicycles were an indispensable feature of base life, and were used by air and ground crew alike to cover the vast distances between the Nissen accommodations scattered around the bases to the mess halls, briefing rooms and dispersal sites like this one. The 92nd acted as a Combat Crew Replacement Centre for 8th Bomber Command and did not fly its first combat mission until 6 September 1943. *Phyllis* had previously served in the 97th Bomb Group, and on 1 May 1943 was assigned to the 303rd Bomb Group at Molesworth. Some 512 B-17Es were built before large-scale production of the famous Fortress really started with the B-17F, which could be distinguished from the B-17E by its moulded Plexiglas nose.

USAF

B-17E 41-9019 *Little Skunkface* of the 414th Bomb Squadron, 97th Bomb Group, in early RAF-style camouflage. This aircraft transferred to the 305th Bomb Group on 6 November 1942, and was later used as a target tug by the 92nd Bomb Group before operating with the 381st Bomb Group for a time in 1943, when it returned to the 92nd Bomb Group in July that year.

USAF via Mike Bailey

B-17F-27-BO 41-24585 *Wulf Hound* of the 360th Bomb Squadron, 303rd Bomb Group, became the first American bomber captured intact when, on 12 December 1942, 1st Lieutenant Paul F. Flickinger was forced to surrender the aircraft at Leeuwarden, Holland, after being attacked by German fighters during a raid on Rouen-Sotteville marshalling yards. *Wulf Hound* was tested at the Luftwaffe Test and Evaluation Centre at Rechlin, and in 1943 was issued to KG 200 for training and clandestine missions.

Hans-Heiri Stapfer

B-17F-27-BO 41-24639 *The Careful Virgin*, which reached the 91st Bomb Group at Bassingbourn early in 1943. The Bassingbourn group, affectionately known as 'Wray's Wragged Irregulars' after its CO, Colonel Stanley T. Wray, flew its first mission on 7 November 1942. *The Careful Virgin* later transferred to the 388th Bomb Group, and was listed MIA on an *Aphrodite* drone mission in 1944.

USAF

On 20 December 1942 at Thurleigh, home of the 367th 'Clay Pigeon' Squadron of the 306th Bomb Group, Maureen Eason, a three-year-old Shirley Temple lookalike, accompanied by a Red Cross welfare worker, visited the base to christen the popular Captain John L. Ryan's B-17F-35-BO 42-5130, 'Sweet Pea'. Maureen lived in a London orphanage and was adopted by the 367th Bomb Squadron as their mascot after Corporal Irvin W. Combs (second from left) and fellow enlisted men collected £101 (over $400) in silver and oversize English pennies, enough to supply the extras for an English orphan for five years. 42-5130, which had the words 'Sweet Pea' stencilled on her nose in anticipation of the christening, flew on the day's mission to Romilly-sur-Seine, France. Ryan encountered strong fighter opposition, however, and he finally returned, on three engines and with a large chunk of wing shot away, at around 3 o'clock, 2½ hours late to keep his date with Maureen. Another B-17 had stood in, and someone dabbed Maureen's fingers with red paint and pressed them onto one of the plane's propeller blades so that the 'Sweet Pea' could be christened in absentia. Three months later, on 6 March 1943, the 'real' *Sweet Pea* failed to return from the raid on Lorient. Ryan, the 367th Squadron Commander elect, evaded capture, was rescued by the French Underground and returned to England on 17 April, only forty-two days after being shot down.

Richards Collection

A tired and haggard Captain Harold Stouse in the 427th Bomb Squadron, 303rd Bomb Group – who piloted B-17F-27-BO 41-24635 *The Eightball* to Wilhelmshaven on 27 January 1943, the first time the 8th Air Force bombed a German target – fills out his flight report after the mission. On 18 March Stouse flew B-17F 41-24561 *The Duchess* home to Molesworth with the body of 1st Lieutenant Jack Mathis, the lead bombardier, on board. Mathis was awarded a posthumous Medal of Honor (the first awarded to an 8th Air Force crew member) for his actions this day on the mission to Vegasack. *The Duchess* was returned to the ZOI by 1 BAD on 6 June 1944.

USAF

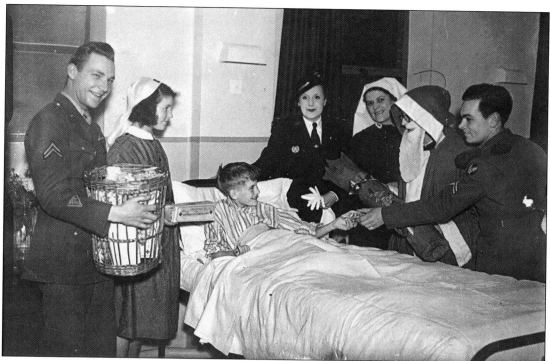

Men of the 306th Bomb Group from Thurleigh, near Bedford, deliver Christmas presents to children in the Bedford County Hospital, Christmas 1942. Barbara Cartland is standing, centre.

*Richards Collection*

The tail unit of B-17F-25-BO 41-24569 of the 427th Bomb Squadron, 303rd Bomb Group, which was shot down by fighters of IV./NJG1 on 4 February 1943. The Fortress, which was flown by Captain L.R. Cole, crashed 8 km north-east of Den Helder in the Waddensee at 11.17 hours.

*Rob de Visser Collection via Theo Boiten*

On 15 February 1943 twenty-one 44th Bomb Group B-24D Liberators attacked Dunkirk. (The 'Flying Eightballs' had arrived in Norfolk from Cheddington, early in October 1942 and flew their first mission one month after the 93rd, on 7 November.) Their target was the *Togo*, a German fighter-control ship. Their long, straight run had enabled the German gunners to determine their speed and height. Flak enveloped the formation, and just as the bomb-release light came on, the lead aircraft, B-24D-5-CO 41-23783 *Betty Anne*, which was piloted by Captain Art V. Cullen with Major Donald W. MacDonald, 67th Squadron CO, took a direct hit. It knocked the roof off the cabin, and blew the cowlings off number two and three engines, which were smoking. For a few moments the noseless bomber flew on, only to fall away to starboard with the port inboard engine aflame and the right inboard ripped from its mounting. Finally, the starboard wing fell off and a huge explosion scattered debris among the formation, hitting another Liberator whose pilot managed to recross the Channel and force-land at Sandwich. MacDonald died later in a German hospital, and Cullen, who was captured, was repatriated in September 1944.

USAF

A line-up of three B-17Fs in the 423rd Bomb Squadron, 306th Bomb Group at Thurleigh. B-17F-5-VE 42-5717 (centre), the first Lockheed Vega-built B-17F, was lost on the mission to St. Nazaire on 16 February 1943 when 1st Lieutenant William H. Warner's crew were shot down. B-17F-40-BO 42-5180 (left) was lost on the 25 June 1943 mission to a target of opportunity at Bremen, when Lieutenant Thomas E. Logan's crew failed to return. B-17F-10-BO 41-24460 was transferred to the 482nd Bomb Group on 22 September 1943.

Richards Collection

The 'Eightballs' taxi out from their muddy dispersals at Shipdham. B-24D-5-CO 41-23818 *Texan II* of the unlucky 67th Bomb Squadron was lost in a mid-air collision with B-24-53-CO 42-40354 *SNAFU* flown by Lieutenant Fred M. Billings Jr, shortly after leaving the coast of England on 16 February 1943, when the target was St. Nazaire. Both aircraft were engulfed in flames, and seconds after impact both exploded, scattering debris even as far as the Fortress formation flying below them. All ten men in Lieutenant John B. Long's crew were killed, while one man survived from Billings' aircraft.

USAF

Captain Howard F. Adams, pilot of B-24D-5-CO 41-23777 *Maisie* in the 66th Bomb Squadron, 44th Bomb Group, was killed when his Liberator was shot down on 26 February 1943 by ace Luftwaffe fighter pilot, Leutnant Heinz Knoke of I./JG1 (below). Only two men survived aboard the Liberator. Among the dead was Robert Perkins Post, a *New York Times* war correspondent, the only one of seven in the 'Writing 69th' who asked to fly with the 44th Bomb Group that day.

via Steve Adams/via Eric Mombeek

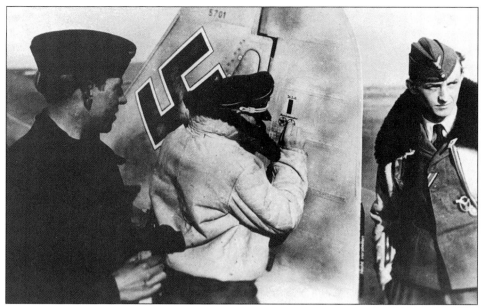

Unteroffizier Heinz Hanke (right) of 9./JG1 waits beside his Focke Wulf 190A-4 as a victory symbol is added for a Liberator he claimed shot down on 26 February 1943. In fact, his 'victim', *Night Raider*, a 93rd Bomb Group Liberator flown by Captain Beattie H. 'Bud' Fleenor, limped back to England to crash-land at Ludham, Norfolk, with a badly wounded crew.

via Eric Mombeek

Traditional 'smoking' of the ceiling of the 306th Bomb Group officers' club at Thurleigh with missions. Major Harry Holt, CO, 367th Bomb Squadron until 4 March 1943 (left); Captain John L. Ryan (with candle); Captain John L. Lambert, 367th Bomb Squadron, later CO, 423rd Bomb Squadron, and Captain George Buckey, 367th CO, 19 August 1943–2 May 1944, lend support. Ryan took command of the 367th on 5 March, and was shot down the next day. He evaded and returned to England after forty-two days. This scene was used later in *12 o'clock High*, which was based on the 306th (the writer, Beirne Lay, evolved the fictional '918th Bomb Group' by multiplying 306 by 3). The 367th Bomb Squadron, which suffered the heaviest losses in 8th Bomber Command during October 1942–August 1943, was nicknamed 'The Clay Pigeons'.

Richards Collection

B-17F-20-BO 41-24504 *The Sad Sack*, one of the original Fortresses assigned to the 91st Bomb Group. Along with sister aircraft 41-24505 *Quitchurbitchin*, *Sad Sack* was the longest-serving of the Bassingbourn group's original Forts. Both were among the first ten 8th Bomber Command B-17Fs to be returned Stateside on 15 March 1943 for training duties.

USAF

B-17F-40-BO 42-5225 *Stormy Weather* of the 323rd Bomb Squadron, 91st Bomb Group, survived an encounter with 8./NJG1 on 4 March, but returned to Bassingbourn with one engine on fire and overshot the runway. The aircraft was repaired and flew again, being renamed *V-Packette* in July 1943, only to be lost on the first Schweinfurt raid on 17 August 1943, when it was flown by 2nd Lieutenant Don Van Der Heyde.

USAF

B-17F-27-BO *We The People*, 41-24614 in the 422nd Bomb Squadron, 305th Bomb Group, at Chelveston, 7 March 1943, with the pilot, Captain Cliff Pyle, far right. In more than thirty missions it never carried exactly the same crew twice, and no crewman was ever wounded. On 8 September 1943 it led the first 8th Air Force night-bombing mission. It survived the war, returning to the ZOI on 31 May 1945.

Cliff Pyle

On 18 March 1943 the 305th Bomb Group, flying at 24,000 ft, placed 76 per cent of its bomb load within 1,000 ft of the MPI (mean point of impact) at Vegasack. It was on this mission that AFCE (Automatic Flight Control Equipment) was used in combat for the first time.

USAF

Air gunners in Lieutenant John H. Murphy's crew of B-24D-1-CO 41-23729 *Shoot Luke* (originally named *Duke*) in the 328th Bomb Squadron, 93rd Bomb Group, Hardwick, England, late March 1943, get their Service Dress, or 'Class A' uniforms ready, to wear on a three-day pass. Technical Sergeant William Mercer, radio operator gunner, writes a letter home, while Staff Sergeant Floyd H. Mabee, engineer top turret gunner, on the bed, sews on a button. Staff Sergeant James Cowan, right waist gunner, reads a newspaper, George Foster, tunnel gunner (standing), does up his tie, while Mahlon Cressey, left waist gunner, shines his shoes. Adam Hastak, tail gunner, ties up his shoe laces. *Shoot Luke* was an original 93rd Bomb Group aircraft

and took part in the early missions from England and North Africa during 1942–3. It was badly shot up on the mission to Vegasack on 18 March, when the original tail gunner, Staff Sergeant Paul B. Slankard, was blasted through the top of his turret by a direct hit from a 20 mm shell. For a moment he flew at 22,500 ft with the upper part of his body protruding from his turret; his left foot, which had caught in the controls, was all that prevented him from being hurled, projectile fashion, through the turret roof. *Shoot Luke* failed to return with a new crew captained by Lieutenant Charles R. Hutchins on 18 October 1943.

USAF

Members of the 93rd Bomb Group, just returned to Hardwick, Norfolk, 24 March 1943, after taking part in the North African campaign, flying from bases in Algeria and Libya, December 1942–late February 1943.

USAF

*Opposite*: Lieutenant Robert M. Cook and crew of B-17F-35-BO 42-32082 of the 728th Bomb Squadron, 452nd Bomb Group, hit by flak, go down in flames on the mission to Châteaudun, France, on 28 March 1943. Incredibly, three men survived to become prisoners of war. The seven other crew were killed.

USAF

Men of the 93rd Bomb Group at mess at Hardwick in April 1943. Because of the sp
for air crews, air crew messed separately from other personnel on base.

Fighter pilots in the 78th Fighter Group leave their briefing room at Duxford, Cambridgeshire. The 78th was based at the famous Battle of Britain station from 3 April 1943, having previously been based at Goxhill, and after first flying the P-38 Lightning, changed to the P-47C Thunderbolt in January 1943.

*via Andy Height*

Staff Sergeant Maynard 'Snuffy' Smith (the first and only enlisted man in the 8th Air Force to receive the Medal of Honor), 306th Bomb Group, emerges from the Harpur Street Register Office in Bedford with his English bride, Mary Rayner. In an attack on St. Nazaire on May Day 1943 the 306th Bomb Group lost six B-17Fs. Lieutenant Lewis P. Johnson Jr's aircraft was hit several times, and it caught fire in the radio compartment and in the tail area. Smith, the ball turret gunner who was on his first mission, hand-cranked his turret back into the aircraft. He climbed out and discovered that the waist gunners and the radio operator had baled out. Smith remained in the aircraft and fought the fire with a hand extinguisher. The Fortress did not show any signs of leaving formation, so Smith assumed the pilots were still on board and went to treat the badly wounded tail gunner. Then he jettisoned the oxygen bottles and ammunition in the radio compartment, manned the waist guns during an attack by enemy fighters, stopping to dampen down the fires and treat the tail gunner. Johnson put the B-17 down at Predannack, near Land's End, after Smith had thrown out all expendable equipment.

Richards Collection

On 13 May 1943 the 1st Wing CO, Brigadier-General Hayward 'Possum' Hansell, flew with the crew of *Dry Martini 4th* in the 364th Bomb Squadron, 305th Bomb Group, to Meaulte. The pilot, Captain Allen V. Martini, is pictured on his return, with Colonel Curtis E. LeMay, his CO, beside him. LeMay worked hard to find the best method of combating fighter attacks without compromising bombing accuracy, and vice versa. After trying 'stacked-up' formations of eighteen aircraft, LeMay finally decided upon staggered three-ship elements within a squadron, and staggered squadrons within a group. Each aircraft manoeuvring for accurate aiming would involve a complicated bombing procedure, so LeMay discarded individual bombing, which had been Standard Operating Procedure (SOP) from the outset, and introduced 'lead crews', whose expert bombardiers signalled to the rest of the formation when to bomb so that all bombs were released simultaneously no matter what position the aircraft were flying. If all the bombs landed a short distance from the MPI, then a target could be destroyed instead of damaged. LeMay's synthesis found support at Wing HQ, where first Brigadier-General Larry Kuter, and later Brigadier-General Hansell, lent encouragement, and gradually lead crews, comprising highly-trained pilots, bombardiers and navigators, became SOP. In the period 1 January 1943–1 October 1943 only 24 per cent of bombs dropped by the 8th Air Force fell within 1,000 ft of the MPI. During 1 October 1943–1 March 1944 it rose to 40 per cent. The USAAF expected to get 40 per cent of its bombs dropped within 500 yards.

USAF via Bill Donald

B-26 Marauders drop in at Bassingbourn, Cambridgeshire, home of the 91st Bomb Group. Originally, four B-26 groups – the 322nd, 323rd, 386th and 387th – joined the 8th Air Force in the summer of 1943, their first mission being flown on 14 May, when eleven B-26Bs of the 322nd Bomb Group from Bury St Edmunds (Rougham) made a raid on the German E-boat base at Ijmuiden in Holland. They missed the target, and flak succeeded in peppering each and every aircraft.

USAF

Major-General George E. Stratemeyer stops to talk with Colonel Leon Johnson, CO, 44th Bomb Group, Major Howard 'Pappy' Moore, and Lieutenant Robert I. Brown by the nose of B-24D-5-CO 41-23817 *Suzy Q* of the 67th Bomb Squadron at Shipdham on 21 April 1943. In the background is B-24D-25-CO 41-24278 *Miss Delores*, which Brown flew with a scratch crew on 14 May 1943 to Kiel. Gilbert 'Gibby' Wandtke, the engineer, was not happy about flying in her as he had been jilted by a girl called Dolores in the States and claimed that *Miss Delores* would probably take them over the target but would not bring them back! He was right. *Miss Delores* was lost in the North Sea after bombing Kiel. Wandtke and Brown survived; three gunners did not.

USAF

Captain Chester 'George' Phillips of the 67th Bomb Squadron, 44th Bomb Group, on a pass in London with English girlfriends. Robert S. Arbib Jr, in his book *Here We Are Together*, graphically described London as 'battered and dirty, worn and scarred, it swarmed with scores of different uniforms, and it spoke in a hundred different tongues. No matter where you were going in the United Kingdom, you had to go through London, and no matter how long you stayed you never saw it all. London was the Babel, the Metropolis, the Mecca. London was It. It had soldiers, sailors, and airmen in uniform, looking for fun. Some were in search of restaurants and theatres. Some were in search of bars and beer. Some were looking for girls. This is London at war, this is England – or a small part of it – with its hair down.' For many, London was the last leave. Phillips was killed over the Kiel shipyards on 14 May, when 8th Bomber Command mounted a series of all out heavy- and medium-bomber raids along the coast of Germany and Holland. He died in one of three explosions which rocked his B-24D-5-CO 41-23807 *Little Beaver* after leaving the target.

Bill Cameron Collection

*Overleaf:* B-24Ds over Kiel, 14 May 1943. The B-17 groups at last got their wish – they flew behind and above the B-24s for the first time in the European Theatre of Operations. This resulted in heavy losses for the Liberators. The 44th's cargo of incendiaries had required a shorter trajectory and a two-mile longer bomb run than the B-17s. Flying a scattered formation, the B-24s were exposed to fighter attack. Altogether, five Liberators were lost, including three belonging to the 67th Bomb Squadron, which brought up the rear of the formation. The first to go down was Lieutenant William Roach and his replacement crew, flying in B-24D-30-CO 42-40126 *Annie Oakley*. There were only two survivors. The 44th Bomb Group was awarded a Distinguished Unit Citation for its part in the Kiel raid, the first made to an 8th Air Force Group.

USAF

B-24D-5-C0 41-23819 *The Rugged Buggy* in the 68th Bomb Squadron, 44th Bomb Group, was one of six Liberators that failed to return from the raid on Kiel. Lieutenant Mac Howell, the pilot, was killed. Sergeant Van Owen was drowned in Kiel Bay despite wearing a Mae West. Major James E. O'Brien, the newly appointed squadron CO, and the surviving members of the crew, were taken prisoners of war. After the Kiel raid there was serious talk of sending home all flying men who had completed fifteen missions. However, their experience was considered vital and they remained on active service.

USAF

Yanks at the Court of King Arthur. On 16 May the Fortress groups were stood down while all available B-24Ds in the 44th and 93rd Bomb Groups were secretly flown to Davidstowe Moor in Cornwall, located near Tintagel Castle, which in Arthurian legend was home to the knights of the Round Table. General Ira Eaker planned to send the B-24s to bomb Bordeaux while the 1st Wing bombed Kiel and the 4th Wing went to Lorient. For some in the 44th Bomb Group, like Major Howard 'Pappy' Moore (right) and Bill Dabney (middle), it was an opportunity to fraternize with locals at nearby Newquay. In the background is the Atlantic Hotel.

via Steve Adams

At 09.00 hours on 17 May Colonel Leon Johnson, General Hodges and the crew of the *Suzy Q*, fitted with four new Twin Wasps following the Kiel debacle, led twenty-one B-24s, followed by eighteen B-24Ds in the 93rd, to Bordeaux. Here, the 44th prepare to taxi out from Davidstowe Moor. The Liberators flew a 700 mile arc over the Atlantic to minimize the chances of enemy detection. Four Liberators were forced to abort with mechanical troubles. Hits were observed on the lock gates at Basin Number One, which collapsed and was flooded by a deluge of water from a nearby river. Direct hits were observed on the Matford aero-engine factory, and the railway yards and chemical works were also hit. One Liberator was forced to seek neutral territory after developing engine trouble shortly before the attack.

via Steve Adams

Meanwhile, fifty-five Fortresses in the 4th Wing had been despatched to the U-boat pens and the power station which served them at Lorient. Six B-17s failed to return. The bombing was described as 'excellent'. The Marauders' diversionary mission to Haarlem and Ijmuiden to bomb targets they had completely missed three days before, on the other hand, was a disaster. All eleven B-26s in the 322nd Bomb Group failed to return. Only twenty crewmen survived to become prisoners of war. By 16 October 1943 all four B-26 medium bomber groups had been assigned to the 9th Air Force, their bases being taken over by B-17s of the 3rd Bomb Division.

USAF

YB-40 gunships like the Vega XB-40 pictured at Burbank, California, in November 1942, made their operational debut on 29 May 1943 when seven in the 92nd Bomb Group took part in a mission for the first time. Intended to provide extra firepower for the beleaguered bomber formations, the YB-40s did not prove successful, as the first weeks of YB-40 operations indicated that the idea of multi-gunned B-17s flying in bomber formations would not work. The additional machine guns on each YB-40 did not add materially to the combined firepower a group formation could provide. Only stragglers were regularly attacked by the Luftwaffe, and the YB-40s were unable to protect these from concentrated attacks. Losses were not made good, although the YB-40s continued flying missions until the end of July 1943.

Boeing

For American servicemen the countryside around the far-flung bases of East Anglia was not so much a culture shock, more a pleasant surprise. In this delightful picture taken by H.E. Bates, three airmen from the 379th Bomb Group stroll down the high street at Kimbolton, seemingly untouched by war. The 379th Bomb Group arrived at the nearby base on 20 May 1943, and flew its first mission just nine days later. It went on to fly more sorties than any other 8th Air Force group, and dropped the greatest bomb tonnage of all of them.

via Bill Donald

Another classic H.E. Bates photo, this one of personnel from Kimbolton, perhaps more than most shows the rapport established between the generous, often homesick 'Yanks' and their young British friends. Airfields completely mingled with farm, field and spinney. Pheasants crowed near the living sites, and rabbits came out in the late evenings. On Sundays, children would stand by the hedgerows and ask, 'Any gum, chum?' The lucky ones were often invited to the base for special occasions or a party.

via Bill Donald

On yer bike, Yank! Cycling, especially 'pubbing missions', became a favourite pastime, and a great escape – albeit temporary – from the horrors of war for many American servicemen. Anyone who had a passion for English literature could not help falling in love with this lovely, pastoral country.

H.E. Bates via Bill Donald

They also serve who only stand and wait. In the control tower at Hardwick these men perform one of their tense jobs – totalling the aircraft returning to their base. Others in the control tower are clearing planes on and off field, handling mid-air traffic, weather forecasting and answering crews' enquiries over the radio. With field glasses is Captain L.L. Lebois, Hoboken, New Jersey, and at the window is Major John K. Strobel, New Orleans, Louisiana.

USAF

A visiting Lockheed P-38 Lightning taxis around the perimeter track at Bassingbourn. The 1st and 14th Fighter Groups were originally assigned to 8th Fighter Command, but were reassigned to the 12th Air Force in September, while the 20th Fighter Group, which flew its first combat mission on 28 December 1943, converted to P-51 Mustangs in July 1944. The 55th Fighter Group flew its first combat mission on 15 October 1943, also converting to the Mustang in July 1944. The 78th Fighter Group flew P-38Gs from December 1942 until February 1943, when it converted to P-47C Thunderbolts.

USAF

The arrival of the British tea van at Hardwick gives 93rd Bomb Group ground personnel the opportunity to relax for a few minutes while they sip steaming cups of the traditional British beverage.

USAF

Pilots in the 84th Fighter Squadron, 78th Fighter Group, pose for the camera at Duxford, June 1943. Major Eugene Roberts, the CO, is second from right, front row. Gene Roberts commanded the 84th Fighter Squadron from August 1942 to 28 September 1943 and was then deputy CO of the Group until 17 December 1943. He flew 89 combat missions with the 78th Fighter Group, during which time he scored nine victories and one probable, all in P-47Cs, like this one. All except two of his victories were achieved flying P-47C-5R-RE 41-6330 *Spokane Chief*. Lieutenant Colonel Roberts commanded the 364th Fighter Group, which was equipped with P-51D Mustangs, from 3 January to November 1945.

via Andy Height

Flight Officer Pete E. Pompetti, pilot of *Darkie* of the 84th Fighter Squadron, 78th Fighter Group, poses for the camera at Duxford with his ground crew. In the background can be seen the RAF married quarters, which, like the airfield, were part of the British expansion plan, and were completed just before the outbreak of war. Fittingly, the dispersal site is occupied by the American Memorial Museum in Great Britain, which was opened officially on 1 August 1997.

via Andy Height

The original crew of B-17F-65-BO *Mr Five By Five* 42-29717 in the 94th Bomb Group, some of whom were missing in action in B-17F-35-DL 42-3190 when pilot Captain Kee Harrison crash-landed the aircraft in a French wheatfield with its bomb load intact after being shot up on the Paris-Le Bourget mission of 14 July 1943. Standing, left to right: Staff Sergeants Jeff Davis Polk, Richard H. Lewis, Jim Curtis, Eino 'Ossie' Asiala, Earl Porath, Charlie McNemar, bombardier. Kneeling: Staff Sergeant Jack Amphlett, Captain Kee Harrison, Lieutenant Martin Stanford, Lieutenant Robert Schaefer. Harrison was assisted by the French Underground, and barefoot, he later crossed the Pyrenees into Spain. Lewis and Ossie Asiala, also aided by the Underground, managed to evade capture until October, before being betrayed and sent to a prisoner of war camp after some uncomfortable Gestapo interrogations. At Stalag Luft VII they were reunited with Curtis and Porath. Later, they heard that Lieutenant David H. Turner (their co-pilot), Polk and Charlie McNemar had travelled with help from the Underground and had returned safely to England. *Mr Five By Five* later flew in the 384th Bomb Group, and was lost on the 25 February 1944 mission to Stuttgart, when it was flown by Lieutenant Kack K. Larsen.

Richard H. Lewis

Officers and enlisted men 'sweating out the mission' at Snetterton Heath. The 96th Bomb Group were first stationed at the Norfolk B-17 base (since the war, a famous motor racing circuit) on 12 June 1943. The British vehicle in the foreground is an indication of the early help the 8th Air Force received from its British ally. Note the RAF liaison officer on the balcony of the control tower.

USAF

*Overleaf:* Major William Wyler, the famous Hollywood director, was sent to England late in 1942 to make a documentary about 8th Air Force operations, principally for American cinema audiences. Filming for the morale-boosting documentary began early in 1943 after bad weather had delayed its start. Five combat photographers were lost aboard B-17s during filming. In the spring of 1943 several B-17s at Bassingbourn were running neck and neck for the honour of being the first to complete twenty-five missions (a combat tour for the crews). One Fortress which caught Wyler's lens more than most, probably because of its emotive and eye-catching name, was the *Memphis Belle* (B-17F-10-BO 41-24485), piloted by Captain Robert K. Morgan. During crew training at Walla Walla, Washington, he had met Miss Margaret Polk of Memphis, Tennessee, who was visiting her sister in Walla Walla. The romance between the pilot and the Memphis girl flourished for a time, but war was no respecter of tradition, and Morgan and Margaret later married other partners. However, the *Belle* would become legendary. The crew flew the twenty-fifth and final mission of their tour on 17 May 1943, to Lorient, and it was duly recorded (using a 'stand-in' B-17F) in 16 mm colour and used with great effect in the documentary. Everyone, it seemed, wanted to meet the famous ten men of the *Memphis Belle*. On 26 May they were introduced to HRH King George VI and Queen Elizabeth at Bassingbourn, and on 13 June Generals Devers and Eaker paid them a visit and then bade them a Stateside farewell to take part in a bond tour of the USA.

USAF

Contrary to popular belief, *Memphis Belle* was not the first heavy bomber to complete an 8th Air Force tour of twenty-five missions. The honour went to B-17F-25-BO 41-24577 *Hell's Angels* in the 303rd Bomb Group on 14 May 1942. After completing forty-eight missions on 19 May, all without ever turning back, it was flown Stateside on 20 January 1944, having been autographed by hundreds of members of the Group at Molesworth, and joined up with original pilot, Captain Irl Baldwin, for a tour of industrial war plants. *The Memphis Belle* finally emerged in April 1945 as a colourful and exciting 38-minute masterpiece which gave American cinemagoers a timely reminder of the grim reality of the war which was being fought at high altitude in the skies over Europe. By this time a tour of missions had risen to thirty-five, and the chances of completing one were even more remote than they had been in 1942/3. Britons saw the film for the first time in the winter of 1944/5.

Lt Col. Harry D. Gobrecht via Brian Maguire

'Hope you gave 'em hell, chum!' Farm workers in this highly evocative photo by H.E. Bates stop to wave as Forts return to their English base after a raid on Germany.

via Bill Donald

*Overleaf:* B-17F of the 366th Bomb Squadron, 305th Bomb Group, over the Huls synthetic rubber plant near Recklinghausen on the edge of the Ruhr on 22 June 1943. The Huls complex was essential to Germany's war effort since its rubber supply in the Far East had been cut off by the Allied blockade. Huls accounted for approximately 29 per cent of Germany's synthetic rubber and 18 per cent of its total rubber supply. Most of the route flown by the 235 B-17s was without escort, so three diversionary raids were flown to try to pull off most of the fighters from the main attacking force, which still had its work cut out coping with the numerous flak guns which made Huls the most heavily defended target in the Reich at this time; 183 B-17s bombed the plant. By the time the bombing was completed smoke from the burning plant was as high as 17,000 ft, and production was curtailed for a month. Full production was not resumed for another five months after that, although fighters and flak brought down 16 B-17s, and another 170 bombers received varying degrees of damage.

USAF

B-17F-85-BO 42-30037 of the 546th Bomb Squadron, 384th Bomb Group, flown by 1st Lieutenant Lykes S. Henderson, is inspected by curious German officers after being shot down on 26 June 1943. This aircraft was an original Group B-17 assigned to the 384th in April 1943 at Sioux City, Iowa.

via Hans-Heiri Stapfer

The wartime caption for this photo of Captain Robert P. Bender of the 336th Bomb Squadron, 95th Bomb Group, read: 'He used up a million dollars worth of Fortresses [all named *Spook*, an unattractive girl in Bender's book] on 15 [sic] missions to German targets. Uncle Sam doesn't mind the expense because Bender has always bombed his targets, always brought his crew home alive, and three times brought back enough of a B-17 to call it "salvage".' The first *Spook*, B-17F-65-BO 42-29704, was written off in a crash-landing at RAF Exeter on 17 May 1943. B-17F-30-DL 42-3176, *Spook II*, and B-17F-30VE 42-5882, *Spook III* (fighter with 2nd Lieutenant Francis J. Regan's crew, 28 July 1942), were so badly shot up that they were salvaged. On 28 June 1943, low on fuel and with an engine shot out over St. Nazaire, Bender ditched B-17-90-BO 42-30226 *Spook #5* 60 miles from England. The crew were finally rescued by Air/Sea Rescue twenty-two hours later. Subsequently, the combat-fatigued pilot, on a visit to a cinema, went berserk when a newsreel showed Fw190s attacking B-17s, and on a test flight take-off in *Spook #5*, Bender froze at the stick. Don Merton, the co-pilot, overpowered him and prevented a crash. Bender never flew #5 again, nor *Spook Six* that followed it. He was hospitalized and returned to America, where he died of a heart attack at the age of twenty-five.

USAF

61

B-17F-95-BO 42-30248 of the 410th Bomb Squadron, 94th Bomb Group, which took the name *The Southern Queen* in July 1943. In August this aircraft joined the 333rd Squadron and became *The Buzzard*, and was later renamed *Prodigal Son*, before finally becoming *Lassie Come Home*. Unfortunately, she did not on 11 January 1944, failing to return with Lieutenant Robert C. Randall's crew, two of whom were killed, and eight made prisoner.

via Geoff Ward

B-17Fs of the 305th Bomb Group warm up engines before take-off from Chelveston for the mission to Villacoublay, France, on 29 June 1943. B-17F-90-BO 42-30155 KY-C was lost on 5 January 1944 with the loss of Percy H. Hoag and crew. B-17F-27-BO 41-24591 *Rigor Mortis* KY-B (left), which was the lead aircraft on the 29 June mission (note the crewman sitting atop the radio hatch opening), was lost on 6 September on the mission to Strasbourg, France, when Raymond E. Holliday's crew went missing in action.

USAF via Bill Donald

B-17F-70-BO 42-29800 *Me and My Gal* returns to runway 06 at Chelveston on three engines after the Villacoublay mission on 29 June. This aircraft was transferred to the 384th Bomb Group at Grafton Underwood, re-coded BK, and was lost on the Schweinfurt mission, 14 October 1943.

USAF via Bill Donald

This photo of B-17Fs of the 305th Bomb Group setting off on a practice mission from Chelveston on 1 July 1943 taken from the control tower shows the airfield still nearing completion.

USAF via Bill Donald

United Service Organization entertainers like French-American Adolph Menjou (centre), reputedly Hollywood's best-dressed man, were in great demand at air bases in East Anglia.

Richards Collection

One of the most famous entertainers to visit England in wartime was undoubtedly Bob Hope, seen here with singer Frances Langford and Tony Romano with the crew of 242 of the 364th Bomb Squadron, 305th Bomb Group at Chelveston in front of B-17F-95-BO 42-30242 *Lallah VIII* on 5 July 1943. His aircraft and crew – which comprised Ellsworth E. Kenyon, pilot; Thomas H. David, co-pilot; John A. Cole, navigator; Joseph F. Collins, bombardier; Findlay J. Mercer, engineer; Russell J. Algren, radio operator (killed in action); Arthur Engelehart, ball turret gunner; Charles M. Green, right waist gunner; Richard W. Lewis, left waist gunner, and Walter Gottshall – was shot down in the mission to Schweinfurt, 14 October 1943.

USAF via Bill Donald

The crew of B-17F-20-DL 42-3049 *Windy City Challenger* of the 305th Bomb Group discuss their experiences upon their return from a mission to Caen on 10 July 1943. Crew, standing, left to right: Thomas H. Seay, pilot (shot down on a night mission); Charles Otis, navigator (missing in action 14 July 1943); Clarence W. Brauser (hands on hips, killed in action 4 October 1943), engineer top turret gunner. Kneeling, left to right: George C. Carruthers, bombardier (missing in action 14 July 1943); John H. Perkins (missing in action 14 July 1943); Bernard Rensicoff, right waist gunner (pointing); Charles B. Cox, radio operator; unknown; unknown. Standing, far right: Joseph P. Deurr and Harold Fedora (leaning against prop).

USAF via Bill Donald

*Windy City Challenger* goes down on the mission to Villacoublay on 14 July 1943 after being raked by cannon fire. The aircraft exploded shortly after, killing seven of the crew, who are buried at Lievesant, south of Paris. Four survivors were blown clear.

USAF via Bill Donald

Anglo-American cooperation in the form of 'gifts for Hitler' at Kimbolton on 20 July 1943. Four days later General Eaker launched Blitz Week, an all-out air offensive on enemy targets throughout Europe. Some 324 B-17s flew a 1,900 mile round trip to Norway and bombed the nitrate works at Heroya and shipping at Trondheim. On 25 July Kiel, Hamburg and Warnemünde were bombed and nineteen B-17s were shot down. Next day over 300 bombers attacked Hanover and Hamburg.

USAF

Blitz Week proved expensive. On 28 July fifteen B-17s were lost on the raid by 120 Fortresses on the Focke Wulf 190 factory at Oschersleben, but production was stopped for a month. On 29 July the shipyards at Kiel and the Heinkel assembly plant at Warnemünde were bombed, and then on 30 July 8th Bomber Command brought down the curtain on Blitz Week when 186 Fortresses from the 1st and 4th Wings went to the Fieseler Werke aircraft factory at Kassel, a round trip of some 600 miles. The weather was fine and P-47 Thunderbolts equipped with long-range fuel tanks escorted the heavies almost to the target and back again. Without the 'Jugs' along, B-17 losses would have been alarming. The Fortress formations were hit by a ferocious onslaught of enemy fighters making pass after pass. Altogether, twelve Fortresses were lost, including *Patches* in the 384th Bomb Group, which crash-landed at the fighter airfield at Boxted. Its parts were used later for other B-17s in the Group. In total, Blitz Week cost Eaker almost 100 aircraft and 90 combat crews.

USAF

Major Eugene Roberts of the 78th Fighter Group. On 28 July 1943, during Blitz Week, Thunderbolts of the 56th and 78th Fighter Groups had carried unpressurized 200 gallon ferry tanks below the centre fuselage for the first time. On 30 July, when they escorted the Fortresses almost to Kassel and back again, flying *Spokane Chief*, Roberts scored the first 'hat trick' of 'kills' (two Fw 190s and a Bf 109), thus becoming the first US pilot to notch a triple victory in Europe.

via Andy Height

Lead navigator Lieutenant Kermit B. Cavedo (far left), in the 369th Bomb Squadron, 306th Bomb Group, at Thurleigh, Bedfordshire, liked the numerical connection between his Squadron and the 'Fightin' 69th' Regiment of the First World War, so, using a little literary licence, he used the name 'Fightin' Bitin' and applied it to the nose of B-17F-50-BO 42-5426. *Fightin' Bitin'* was one of four 306th Bomb Group B-17s lost during the raid on Kiel on 29 July 1943, when it carried 1st Lieutenant Donald R. Winter's crew, but both the name and the emblem, showing two insects sparring, were adopted by the 369th Bomb Squadron. Its sister squadron, the 367th, which had the heaviest losses in 8th Bomber Command during October 1942–August 1943, was nicknamed the 'Clay Pigeons'.

Richards Collection

Worth fighting for. Major Urzal P. Harvel, 44th Bomb Group photographer at Shipdham, stands in front of the camera for a change to be pictured with this pretty young English miss.

via Steve Adams

P-47C Thunderbolts 41-6234 *Sugar Baby* and *Little Cookie* of the 62nd Fighter Squadron, 56th Fighter Group, pictured away from their home base, at Shipdham, in the summer of 1943.

Bill Cameron Collection

In the summer of 1943 three 8th Air Force B-24 groups – 44th (B-24D-15-CO 41-24009 'W' *Margaret Ann*, which was subsequently re-assigned to the 98th Bomb Group, in October 1943, pictured), 93rd and 389th – were dispatched to North Africa to lend weight to the invasion of Sicily. On 20 July 1943 these three groups, and two 9th Air Force Liberator groups, were withdrawn from the campaign in Italy, and began twelve days' training for TIDAL WAVE (the codename for the attack on oilfields at Ploesti, 1 August 1943) with practice flights against a mock-up target in the desert. On 6 July General Lewis Brereton, the overall commander, had told his five group commanders that a low-level, daylight attack would be made on Ploesti to achieve maximum surprise and ensure the heaviest possible damage in the first attack. Brereton had studied target folders for two weeks before making his decision. Most of the crews were apprehensive. This was no ordinary mission, and morale was not improved when Brereton told them that losses were expected to be as high as 50 per cent.

Dexter Hodge via Steve Adams

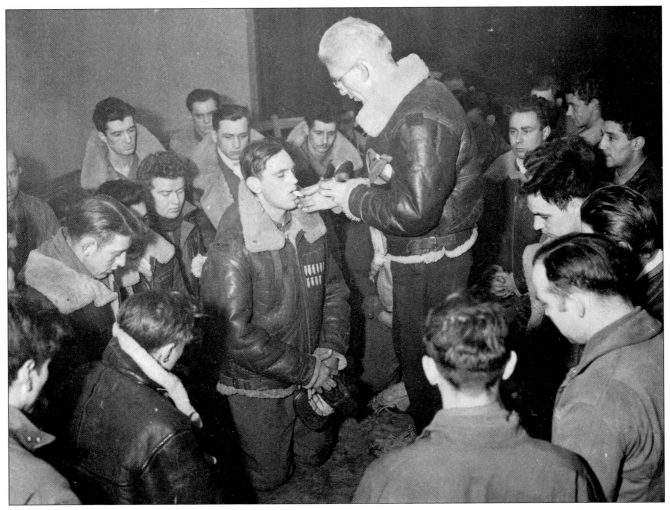

Father Gerald Beck, the Catholic chaplain at Hethel, who joined the 389th Bomb Group in North Africa, distributes communion to his combat crews after a mission briefing. Driving in his jeep, named 'Hellzapoppin'', at top speed, he would go from B-24 to B-24, making sure that no one was denied communion. In North Africa, Father Beck was inside a B-24 administering the sacrament at take-off time and ended up giving Holy Communion in the air during the mission! He flew a number of missions, earning the Air Medal, in order, he claimed, better to understand what the men had to endure, until, eventually, the head chaplain in Europe put a stop to his flying career. Father Beck was probably the most influential driving force behind the men of the 389th Bomb Group.

USAF

B-24D Liberators over the Ploesti oilfields, 1 August 1943. Of the 177 B-24s which had set out, 167 had actually attacked their targets and had dropped 311 tons of bombs on the refineries. Some 54 B-24Ds were lost over the targets, and 3 more crashed at sea; 7 B-24D crews were interned in Turkey, while 19 had landed in Cyprus Of the 92 that returned to North Africa, 55 had varying degrees of battle damage.

via Steve Adams

B-24Ds leaving the target at very low level, 1 August 1943. Despite the great sacrifice, the Liberators had only destroyed 42 per cent of the plants' refining capacity and 40 per cent of its cracking capacity. Most of the refineries were repaired, and within a month were operating at pre-mission capacity again. This led to repeated attempts to destroy the plants, and the USAAF would lose in excess of 200 more bombers and over 2,000 further aircrew in raids on the Ploesti refineries before the end of the war in Europe.

via Steve Adams

B-24Ds of the 506th Bomb Squadron leave the burning pyre that was Ploesti, 1 August 1943.

Pete Frizzell via Steve Adams

*Suzy Q* of the 67th Bomb Squadron, 44th Bomb Group, reposes in the North African desert at Benina Main, Libya, during the Eightballs' first African campaign. On the Ploesti raid she was used as the lead aircraft and was piloted by Major Bill Brandon with Colonel Leon Johnson, CO, 44th Bomb Group, in the right-hand seat. Note the rudder, which was damaged on the raid. *Suzy Q* was one of eight Liberators in the 44th Bomb Group which failed to return from a raid on Foggia, Italy, on 16 August. 1st Lieutenant Walter R. Bateman and crew were all killed in action.

Bill Cameron Collection

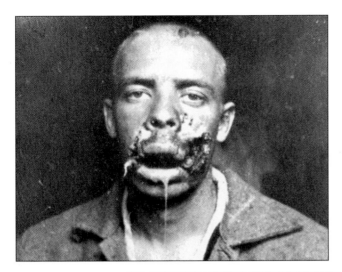

1st Lieutenant Henry Lasco, pilot of B-24D-20-CO 41-24153 *Sad Sack II* in the 66th Bomb Squadron, 44th Bomb Group, in a Romanian prisoner of war camp. A 20 mm shell fired from a Bf 109 passed through both his cheeks and his palate. It was his seventh mission. Both he and his co-pilot, Lieutenant Joe Kill, came from Chicago. Five of the crew, including Thomas M. Wood, the tail gunner, Sergeant Leonard Raspotnik, who died on the way to hospital, and Sergeant Joe Spivey, who was hit in the stomach, were killed.

via Elmer Reinhart

General Leon W. Johnson MoH (left) sits with 1st Lieutenant Henry Lasco (centre, apparently none the worse for wear except a scar on his left cheek) and other 44th Bomb Group veterans of Ploesti following their return to Shipdham in September 1944 after a year in a Romanian prisoner of war camp. The three men on the right were part of 1st Lieutenant Elmer Reinhart's crew in B-24D-53-CO 42-40371 *GI Gal*, the last B-24 away from Blue target. Part of the wing was shot off, and Bf109s shot away most of the tail turret, but Staff Sergeant George Van Son emerged alive from the debris. Eighty miles from the target all the crew, except Flight Officer Charles L. Starr, the co-pilot, whose parachute failed to open properly, baled out safely.

Elmer Reinhart via John Page

On 1 August 1943 Major James T. Posey, a West Pointer from Henderson, Kentucky (who succeeded Leon Johnson as Group CO at Shipdham on 3 September 1943), led twenty-one B-24s in a very accurate strike on 'Blue I', Creditul Minier Brazi, 5 miles south of Ploesti. Only two of Posey's twenty-one Liberators were lost, and Creditul Minier was put out of commission for the rest of the war.

Bill Cameron Collection

The funeral of Captain Robert C. Mooney, 389th Bomb Group pilot killed on the Ploesti raid, at Izmir, Turkey, on 2 August 1943. The refinery at Steaua Romana, Campina, code-named 'Red Target', was bombed by the 389th Bomb Group and totally destroyed at a cost of six of the Sky Scorpions' twenty-nine Liberators, and put out of production for six years. Left to right: Lieutenant Harold L. James, pilot; Staff Sergeant John P. Morris, James' waist gunner; next, 2nd row, Lieutenant Rocky Triantafellu, Mooney's bombardier; unknown; next, 2nd row, Lieutenant James F. Gerrits, Mooney's co-pilot; Staff Sergeant Elvin H. Henderson, Mooney's tail gunner; Staff

Sergeant Max C. Cavey, James' top turret gunner (behind); Technical Sergeant Harold M. Thompson, James' engineer; Staff Sergeant Grover A. Edminston, James' bombardier (behind); Staff Sergeant Hugh R. McLaren, James' waist gunner/assistant radio operator; Technical Sergeant Earl L. Zimmerman (behind McLaren) James' radio operator; Staff Sergeant Robert L. Hamilton, James' tail gunner; Lieutenant William R. Gilliat, James' navigator; unknown; Lieutenant Robert W. Schwellinger, James' co-pilot.

Hugh R. McLaren Collection

Colonel (later General) Leon W. Johnson, CO, 44th Bomb Group, a 39-year-old West Pointer who led his group on the Ploesti low-level mission to 'White V' – Columbia Aquila. The refinery was put out of production for eleven months. On 17 August Johnson was awarded the Medal of Honor, America's highest military award, which was presented to him at a ceremony at Shipdham on 22 November, by which time he commanded the 14th Combat Wing. Every crew member on Ploesti received the DFC, and all five groups received Presidential Unit Citations. Four other Medals of Honor were awarded, to Lieutenant Lloyd 'Pete' D. Hughes (posthumous) of the 389th Bomb Group, Colonel John 'Killer' Kane, CO, 98th Bomb Group; Colonel Addison T. Baker, CO (posthumous), and Major John 'The Jerk' Jerstad, 93rd Bomb Group (posthumous).

Dexter Hodge Collection

Howard F. Gotts and Elvin L. Phillips from 1st Lieutenant George W. Winger's crew in the 44th Bomb Group photographed just prior to the Ploesti mission, 1 August 1943. B-24D-15-CO 41-24015 *Wing Dinger* was a borrowed 376th Bomb Group aircraft. It pulled straight up and then fell out of the sky. Two doll-like figures popped out of the waist windows, barely 200 or 300 ft above the ground (Staff Sergeants Michael J. Cicon and 17-year-old Bernard G. Traudt), and miraculously survived. Gotts and Phillips were among the dead.

Will Lundy via Steve Adams

One of the lucky ones. Staff Sergeant Hugh R. McLaren, Lieutenant Harold L. James' waist gunner/assistant radio operator in the 389th Bomb Group on the Ploesti raid, pictured with his wife.

Hugh McLaren Collection

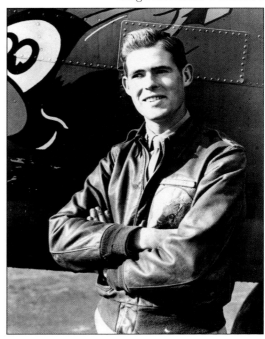

Major (later Colonel, 67th Bomb Squadron, 44th Bomb Group, CO) Bill Cameron, pictured in front of a B-24D at Shipdham. Bill flew many missions for the 'Eightballs', including the low-level strike on the Columbia Aquila refinery at Ploesti on 1 August 1943 in B-24D-25-CO 41-24229 *Buzzin Bear*, a reference to his home state of California. The *Bear* was one of eight Liberators in the 44th Bomb Group which failed to return from a raid on Foggia, Italy, on 16 August, when it carried 1st Lieutenant Leighton C. Smith and his crew.

Colonel William Cameron Collection

Back home from Ploesti. B-24D-1-CO 41-23711 *Jerk's Natural*, which was flown on the first five missions by Lieutenant John 'The Jerk' Jerstad, who was awarded a posthumous Medal of Honor for his action at Ploesti, pictured on its return to Hardwick, England, from North Africa, still sporting its RAF theatre fin flashes.

USAF

Another Ploesti survivor was B-24D-1-CO 41-23667 *Ball of Fire*, of the 93rd Bomb Group, seen here in the livery of the Hardwick Group's assembly aircraft in the less fraught skies of Norfolk, late in 1943.

USAF

Captain Jack Dieterle and co-pilot, Flight Officer Thomas Baum of the 389th Bomb Group, flew their last mission, to Ploesti, on 1 August 1943, in B-24D-90-CO CO 42-40722 *The Little Gramper*. Dieterle became operations officer and Baum got his own crew. Captain Ben Walsh and his co-pilot, Sam Blessing, took over the *Gramper* and her crew after losing their B-24D over the Straits of Messina near Sicily. Both were rescued by Sicilian fishing boats and returned to Benghazi. Tom Campbell, the crew's navigator, originally called the reptiles in the African desert 'Grampers', from which the aircraft got its name. Campbell was killed in a plane crash in Sweden early in 1944. Here, Lieutenant Colonel Tom Conroy congratulates Walsh after finishing his last mission for him as squadron commander.

Russ D. Hayes Collection

B-17F-30-BO 42-5077 DF:T *Delta Rebel 2* of the 324th Bomb Squadron, 91st Bomb Group, in flight in the summer of 1943.

USAF via Mike Bailey

The *Rebel* is awarded the Air Medal by pilot Lt George Birdsong, who safely completed his tour in this aircraft. On 12 August, when 330 heavies bombed targets in the Ruhr, *Delta Rebel 2* was one of twenty-five bombers which went missing in action, with the loss of 2nd Lieutenant Robert W. Thompson and crew.

USAF

B-17 Flying Fortresses of the 385th Bomb Group in the 4th Wing cross the aircraft plant at Regensburg on 17 August 1943, part of an ambitious and daring strike to mark the anniversary mission of the 8th Air Force, which also saw the 1st Wing head for the ball-bearing plant at Schweinfurt, led by Brigadier-General Robert Williams. To minimize attacks from enemy fighters, Colonel Curtis E. LeMay's 4th Wing B-17s flew on to North Africa after the target. The 1st Wing, meanwhile, flew a parallel course to Schweinfurt to confuse the enemy defences further before returning to England after the raid.

via Ian McLachlan

The 91st head for home and Bassingbourn. On 17 August the 1st Wing lost thirty-six Fortresses. Hardest hit in the 1st Wing were the 381st and 91st Bomb Groups, which lost eleven and ten B-17s respectively.

USAF

B-17F-100-BO 42-30372 *Shack Rabbit III*, and B-17F-85-BO 42-30130, of the 96th Bomb Group crossing the Brenner Pass after the raid on Regensburg, 17 August 1943. Colonel Curtis E. LeMay, the 4th Wing CO, flying aboard Captain Tom Kenney's B-17F-100-BO *Fertile Myrtle III*, 42-30366, in the 338th Bomb Squadron, led the raid. Although the Snetterton Heath group did not lose a single B-17, the 4th Wing lost twenty-four aircraft, while sixty Fortresses which made it to North Africa had to be left behind for repairs. *Fertile Myrtle III* was badly shot up over Bremen on 16 December 1943 and crashed near Norwich after being abandoned over Norfolk by Kenney's crew.

via Geoff Ward

A crew from the 339th Bomb Squadron, 96th Bomb Group, leaving their B-17F-100-BO 42-30359 after arriving safely in North Africa after the Regensburg mission on 17 August 1943. This aircraft, and the crew of 2nd Lieutenant Linwood D. Langley, was lost over Oldenburg on 29 November 1943 on the mission to Bremen, when German fighters shot the aircraft in two. Only the navigator and the tail gunner survived.

via Geoff Ward

B-17F-95-BO 42-30325 *Miss Carry* of the 570th Bomb Squadron, 390th Bomb Group, over the Alps on 17 August 1943. Some 376 Fortresses bombed the aircraft plants at Regensburg and the ball-bearing plant at Schweinfurt; sixty B-17s were shot down; almost three times as many as the previous highest total, on 13 June, when twenty-six bombers were lost. *Miss Carry* was involved in a mid-air collision near Hamelin, Germany, with B-17 42-30334 *Virgin Sturgeon* on 29 January 1944. Lieutenant William J. Harding's crew were all made prisoners of war. *Miss Carry* returned safely. After another mishap, it was salvaged on 2 May 1944.

via Ian McLachlan

B-17F-20-BO 41-24524 *The Eagle's Wrath* of the 323rd Bomb Squadron, 91st Bomb Group, which was lost on 17 August 1943 when it was flown by Lieutenant Anth━━ ━━ ━━ ━━ ━━ ━━━ty-seven B-17s in the First Division were so badly damaged that they never flew again.

USAF

Colonel Curtis E. LeMay (left), CO, 4th Wing, who led his formation to Regensburg and on to North Africa on 17 August 1943. The surviving 128 B-17s, some flying on three engines and many trailing smoke, were attacked by a few fighters on the way to the Alps. LeMay circled his formation over Lake Garda to try to give the cripples a chance to rejoin the Wing. Third highest loss of the day belonged to the 100th Bomb Group in the 4th Wing, which lost nine Fortresses.

via Ian McLachlan

Lieutenant Robert Wolf's *Wolf Pack* (centre) and other 100th Bomb Group B-17s head for North Africa after the 17 August raid on Regensburg. Wolf's aircraft (42-30061) received 20 mm cannon fire to the tail fin, and a life raft released hit the left tail plane. Top aircraft is *Laden Maiden* (42-5861), flown by Lieutenant Owen D. 'Cowboy' Roane. Wolf and Roane managed to reach North Africa; nine other 100th Bomb Group Fortresses did not. *Laden Maiden* failed to return from a raid on 30 December 1943 with Lieutenant Marvin Leininger's crew. Only the bombardier and navigator survived, and successfully evaded capture; the rest were killed in action. *Wolf Pack* had a better fate, being returned to the Zone of the Interior on 28 June 1944.

Thorpe Abbotts Memorial Museum

Lieutenant Donald Oakes' B-17F-85-BO *High Life* (42-30080), belonging to the 100th Bomb Group, was the first B-17 to land in Switzerland. A 20 mm shell exploded in the number three engine on 17 August 1943 on the raid on Regensburg, and Oakes had to land wheels-up at Dubendorf, a military airfield near Zurich. Two B-17s in the 390th Bomb Group had been shot down in the target area, and a third, out of fuel, headed for Spain. It landed near Toulon in France and the crew were made prisoners of war. An unidentified Fortress crash-landed in northern Italy, and five more eventually ditched in the Mediterranean.

Hans-Heiri Stapfer

Returning from North Africa on 24 August 1943, the B-17s of the Third Division bombed the airfield at Bordeaux-Merignac en route to England. B-17F *The Miracle Tribe* of the 96th Bomb Group, flown by Lieutenant Miracle, was the first to land at Snetterton Heath, carrying 'Lady Moe', a sloe-eyed Algerian donkey (pictured with gunners, Louis Klimchak and Coots Matthews), which travelled back in the radio room with a long-nosed oygen mask attached, and blankets to keep her warm. 'Lady Moe' was killed by a train on the nearby LNER railway line on the morning of 3 October 1945 and was buried on the base.

Coots Matthews via Geoff Ward

56th Fighter Group pilots strike up a pose for the cameraman. Standing, left to right: Dave 'The Silver Fox' Robinson, Intelligence Officer; Al Davis; Handley Sayers. Front: Gordon Batdorf; Walt Moore; James Peppers; Ray Petly; Roger Dyar; Glen Schiltz and John Vogt. Schiltz downed three Fw190s on 17 August 1943, and Vogt bagged one on 2 September 1943.

56th Fighter Group WWII Association via Alan Hague

B-17F-60-BO 42-29557 *Yankee Girl* X:KO of the 305th Bomb Group at Chelveston, 22 August 1943. This aircraft transferred to the 384th Bomb Group at Grafton Underwood and was re-coded SO:S. Piloted by 2nd Lieutenant William E. Kopf, it crash-landed at RAF Desford on 10 October 1943, hitting a hangar.

USAF via Bill Donald

B-17F-15-VE *Bomb-Boogie*, 42-5763, in the 401st Bomb Squadron, 91st Bomb Group, in flight. On 6 September 1943 this Fortress, flown by 1st Lieutenant Elwood D. Arp's crew, was one of forty-five heavies shot down when 338 B-17s targeted the aircraft components factories at Stuttgart. Cloud interfered with assembly over England and prevented accurate bombing at the target. Brigadier-General Robert B. Travis, who had assumed command of the 1st Wing from Brigadier-General Williams, circled Stuttgart for approximately thirty minutes in a vain attempt to find the target, but the 262 heavies were forced to bomb targets of opportunity instead.

USAF

B-17F-25-VE 42-5841 of the 306th Bomb Group landed in Switzerland on 6 September 1943, at Magadino airfield, when it was piloted by Flight Officer David W. Bees. It was later flown to the Emmen test and experimental centre, and at the end of the war Swiss ground crews performed an engine exchange before the aircraft was handed back to the USAAF.

Hans-Heiri Stapfer

B-17F-10-DL 42-3002 BN:Z *The Old Squaw*, which joined the 359th Bomb Squadron, 303rd Bomb Group, at Molesworth, 8 April 1943, the day that Lieutenant (later Captain) Claude W. Campbell's (standing, left) crew made their first training flight. To his right are: Miller, Ririe, and William A. Boutelle, bombardier. Kneeling: Howard E. Hernan, top turret gunner; Wilson, Quick, Kraft, Backert. *The Old Squaw* went missing in action on 6 September 1943 when it was ditched in the North Sea. Lieutenant Robert J. Hullar and crew were rescued.

Howard Hernan Collection

B-17F-10-VE 42-5729 of the 401st Bomb Squadron, 91st Bomb Group, taking off from Bassingbourn late in 1943. This aircraft originally served with the 306th Bomb Group at Thurleigh, from 18 February 1943 to 7 September 1943. It was returned to the USA in March 1944.

USAF

B-24H-1-FO 42-7466 'N' *Ford's Folly*, a 578th Bomb Squadron, 392nd Bomb Group Liberator, one of the first H's to roll off the production line at Willow Run, is being refuelled at Wendling on 9 September 1943 for the Group's first combat mission. The Group was equipped with new B-24H and B-24J Liberators fitted with power-operated nose gun turrets. Three days earlier, on 6 September, some sixty-nine Liberators, including the 392nd, flew a diversionary sweep over the North Sea for the Fortresses attacking Stuttgart. *Ford's Folly* was salvaged on 31 January 1944, repaired, and failed to return on 11 September 1944.

USAF

B-17F-100-BO 42-30362 *Wee Bonnie II* of the 561st Bomb Squadron, 388th Bomb Group, releases its bomb load on target. *Wee Bonnie II* and Lieutenant Adalbert D. Porter's crew failed to return on 9 September 1943, when a record 330 heavies were despatched to targets in France. Flak and a 20 mm shell hit the B-17 on the bomb run over Paris, creating a large hole in the wing near the number one engine. Bombs were jettisoned and the crew baled out, the aircraft crashing at Houilles. Five crew evaded capture, the other six were captured and made prisoners of war.

USAF

B-17F-110-BO 42-30607 *Pat Hand*, of the 337th Bomb Squadron, 96th Bomb Group, flown by Lieutenant Ken E. Murphy, takes a direct flak hit over Paris just after bombs-away during the raid on the Hispano-Suiza aero-engine assembly plant on 15 September 1943. During the bomb run one other 96th Bomb Group Fortress was sent spinning down and on fire after being shot up by a fighter; Lieutenant Richardson's B-17 was hit by flak, and his aircraft exploded.

USAF

B-17F-70-BO *Rebel's Revenge* 42-29750, an ex-96th Bomb Group Fortress which replaced *Delta Rebel 2* in the 323rd Bomb Squadron, 91st Bomb Group, on 24 August 1943. *Rebel's Revenge* was lost over Holland on 27 September 1943, when it was flown by 1st Lieutenant John M. Perritt.

USAF

B-17F-115-BO 42-30647 *Polly Ann* of the 305th Bomb Group en route to Stuttgart on 6 September 1943. The mission lasted seven hours, of which five hours were on oxygen. This aircraft crashed from 2,000 ft over Chelveston airfield on 23 September 1943. Norman A. Brouin, the pilot, liked to sit in co-pilot Walter H. Menziel's seat during landing, and it is believed that while swopping positions, someone accidentally activated the autopilot. *Polly Ann* plunged to the ground, striking two other B-17s on the way down (they managed to land safely). There were no survivors from Brouin's crew.

USAF via Bill Donald

B-17s of the 94th Bomb Group en route to Emden on 27 September 1943. The nearest Fortress is B-17F-75-DL 42-3538 *Ten Knights In a Bar Room*, which failed to return from Wesel, Germany, with Lieutenant Dennis T. Carlson's crew on 4 October 1943. Six of the crew evaded capture, the other four were captured and made prisoners of war.

USAF via Cliff Hatcher

B-17F-25-DL 42-3082 *Double Trouble* of the 333rd Bomb Squadron, 94th Bomb Group. The pilot, Lieutenant Bill Winnesheik, aborted the mission to Bremen on 25 June 1943 after fighters knocked out two engines, and he landed in England despite a full bomb load. On 4 October 1943, during a mission to St. Dizier, France, fighters knocked out the number three engine and the propeller refused to feather, but the crew managed to crash-land at Margate. Vance Van Hooser, the assistant engineer waist gunner, who was on his 23rd mission, was hit in the head by 20 mm shell fragments and never flew again.

USAF

B-17s of the 388th Bomb Group, 3rd Bomb Division, crossing Bremen on 8 October 1943 at 23,000 ft. The target below is obscured effectively by German smoke pots. None of the 23 B-17s despatched from Knettishall were lost, but 21 were damaged by flak from the 260 AA guns at Bremen. After the P-47 escort had withdrawn, low on fuel, the B-17 divisions were met in strength, and the unfortunate 381st Bomb Group, flying as low group in the First Division formation, lost 7 of its 18 B-17s, including the lead aircraft. Altogether, the 8th lost 26 bombers, including 14 from the Third Division, 7 of them from the 'Bloody Hundredth'.

USAF

Smoke trails from B-17F-100-BO 42-30377 *Roger The Lodger II*, of the 412th Bomb Squadron, 95th Bomb Group, shortly before it went down in flames in Dutch territorial waters with Lieutenant Ralph W. Eherts' crew on the Marienburg mission, 9 October 1943. On this day 378 heavies were despatched to three targets, 115 aircraft from the 1st and 41st Combat Wings going to the Arado aircraft component plant at Anklam, near Peenemünde, as a diversion for 263 bombers attacking the port of Gydnia and the Focke Wulf plant at Marienburg (the Anklam force lost fourteen B-17s, all from the 1st Combat Wing). Fighters scored hits in the number two engine aboard *Roger The Lodger II*, and put a rocket in the number three engine. Seven of Ehert's crew baled out, but two of the parachutes were on fire. The five survivors perished in the freezing waters of the North Sea. Robert Wing, the bombardier, had a premonition the night before that he would not return.

USAF

B-17F-50-DL 42-3352 *Virgin's Delight* of the 94th Bomb Group, piloted by Lieutenant R.F. 'Dick' LePore of the 410th lead squadron, photographed by Captain Ray D. Miller, the 410th Squadron Flight Surgeon leaving the burning Fw 190 factory at Marienburg on 9 October 1943. On the bomb run Le Pore was not using oxygen, and was in fact eating a Mars bar from his PX rations! The target was completely demolished. Anti-aircraft defences were thought unnecessary to defend a target so far from England, which allowed the heavies to bomb from 11,000–13,000 ft. At these heights accuracy was almost guaranteed: 60 per cent of the bombs dropped by the 96 Fortresses exploded within 1,000 ft of the MPI, and 83 per cent fell within 2,000 ft. Before the raid the Marienburg plant had been turning out almost 50 per cent of the Luftwaffe's Fw 190 production. General Eaker called it a 'classic example of precision bombing'. *Virgin's Delight* and 2nd Lieutenant Walter Chyle's crew failed to return on 29 November 1943, when the aircraft was ditched in the North Sea with the loss of all the crew.

USAF

B-17F-60-DL 42-3426 *Kemy II* of the 571st Bomb Squadron, 390th Bomb Group, formerly *Spider* and *Kemy Jr. Kemy II*, with Lieutenant William W. Smith's crew, was one of eight in the 390th Bomb Group which failed to return from Münster on Sunday 10 October, where for the first time in the war the 8th Air Force bombed a residential area to deprive the Germans of its rail workers. Three of the crew were killed in action, the other seven survived to be made prisoners of war. It was a black day for the 13th Wing as a whole, which lost 25 of the 29 B-17s lost by the Third Division. Worst-hit was the 100th Bomb Group, which lost 12 bombers. This brought its total loss to 19 in three days. In all, 88 bombers had been lost on three successive days, and the losses came at a time when intelligence sources revealed that Luftwaffe fighter strength was on the increase.

*via Ian McLachlan*

B-17F-35-BO 42-5086 *Wahoo II*, one of nine replacement Forts received by the 306th Bomb Group, late in November 1942, in flight near Luton, close to the LMS Bedford–London railway line. The original pilot, Captain Robert 'Rip' P. Riordan, 369th Bomb Squadron (from 10 July 1944, the Squadron CO), brought the badly battle-damaged aircraft back from Lille on 8 November 1942. She was badly damaged again on the mission to Heroya, Norway, on 24 July 1943, when Captain David H. Wheeler, who was on his last mission, brought her back to Thurleigh with a badly wounded navigator (who never flew again) and injured tail gunner. The Fort was repaired, and on 5 September transferred to the 546th Bomb Squadron, 384th Bomb Group. *Wahoo II* crashed on the bank of the River Dove at Eye returning from Münster on 10 October with 2nd Lieutenant William M. Wilson's crew, who abandoned the aircraft near Ipswich.

Richards Collection

B-17F *Gremlin Trainer* of the 305th Bomb Group pictured at Chelveston on 13 October 1943.

USAF via Bill Donald

B-17F-115-BO 42-30727 piloted by Lieutenant William C. Bisson in the 367th 'Clay Pigeons' Bomb Squadron, 306th Bomb Group, was one of ten Fortresses the Thurleigh Group lost on 14 October 1943 when Brigadier-General Orvil Anderson, Commanding General of 8th Bomber Command, sent his bombers to Schweinfurt. Bad weather wrecked the timetable, and losses were heavy. Flak knocked out two of Bisson's engines, and fighters riddled the rear fuselage, killing Staff Sergeant Thompson E. Wilson, the tail gunner. Only 2nd Lieutenant Charles R. Stafford, the co-pilot (who exited through the side cockpit window), and four crewmen in the aft section escaped death.

Richards Collection

Flak 'thick enough to walk on'. B-17s of the 306th Bomb Group weave their way through a heavy barrage over Schweinfurt on 14 October 1943. Altogether, the First Division lost 45 Fortresses, with the 305th Bomb Group losing 16 aircraft alone. The Third Division lost 15 aircraft. Of the bombers which returned to England, 142 in both divisions were damaged. Seventeen B-17s crashed in England as a result of their battle-damaged condition or were so badly damaged that they had to be written off. Of the returning bombers, 121 required repairs, and another five fatal casualties and forty-three wounded crewmen were removed from the aircraft.

Richards Collection

B-17F-70-BO 42-29803 led a chequered career in the 8th. Originally it was assigned to the 95th Bomb Group before moving to the 305th Bomb Group on 17 June 1943, and later, the 306th Bomb Group (pictured). This aircraft was then assigned to the 381st Bomb Group on 11 September 1943, and was the only Group aircraft that failed to return from the Schweinfurt mission, 14 October 1943.

USAF via Bill Donald

B-17F-15-DL 42-3037 *Windy City Avenger* was christened as a publicity stunt after the loss of *Windy City Challenger*, on the mission to Villacoublay on 14 July 1943 (both pilots, John Perkins and Harry Task, having come from Chicago). *Windy City Avenger* was transferred to the 384th Bomb Group and was lost returning from the raid on Schweinfurt, 14 October 1943.

via Bill Donald

General Maurice 'Mo' Preston, CO, 379th Bomb Group, listens to Major 'Rip' Rohr upon his return as leader of the Group during the disastrous mission to Schweinfurt on 14 October 1943. Preston noted that Rohr 'looked harassed, shaken and more agitated than I had ever seen him'.

USAF

A respite from bombing. American combat crews play softball with their RAF allies while formations of Liberators return from bombing targets in enemy-occupied Europe.

USAF

B-17F-5-VE 42-39843, *Dailey's Mail*, seen here over California on a Lockheed-Vega Company test flight, was one of the replacements assigned to the 364th Bomb Squadron, 305th Bomb Group, at Chelveston on 16 October 1943. She was reassigned to the Night Leaflet Squadron on 23 May 1944. Altogether, Lockheed-Vega built 2,250 B-17Gs at their Burbank factory during the Second World War, in addition to 500 B-17Fs.

Lockheed

B-17Fs 42-30793 *Tom Paine* (left) and 42-30317 *Second Chance* (right) prepare to take off from Knettishall on 20 October 1943. *Second Chance* and 2nd Lieutenant William H. McGowan's crew, who were on their first mission, were lost on the raid on Bremen, 26 November 1943. It was the aircraft's fortieth mission. Returning from Krezinki, Poland, on 11 April 1944, Lieutenant McWhite crash-landed *Tom Paine* at Beccles with three wounded on board. The aircraft was salvaged on 2 June 1945. In all, this Fort flew ninety-two missions. *Second Chance* went MIA on 26 November 1943 with 2nd Lieutenant William H. McGowan and crew on their first mission. Some reports suggest that it was involved in a mid-air collision with a 401st Bomb Group B-17; the latter managed to make it back to Detling, where it was salvaged.

USAF

Something to sing about. USAAF and RAF personnel strike up a song for the benefit of the cameraman at Kimbolton, 27 October 1943, when the 8th Air Force was grounded.

USAF

P-47s escort B-17s of the 94th Bomb Group to Münster on 11 November 1943. Only 58 heavy bombers of the Third Bomb Division attacked, 111 others having to abort because of bad weather during assembly (which also led the 175 B-17s of the First Bomb Division having to abort their mission to Wesel while over the English Channel). Those that got to Münster concentrated on the marshalling yards.

USAF via Cliff Hatcher

B-17Fs of the 95th Bomb Group over Wilhelmshaven in November 1943. Nearest aircraft is B-17F-30-DL 42-3153 *Devil's Daughter*, which returned to the ZOI on 9 April 1944.

USAF

An American who was well known to the moviegoing public in the USA and Britain before the war was gangling 6 ft 4 in actor James Maitland Stewart. Born of Scottish-Irish parents on 20 May 1908 in Indiana, Pennsylvania, where his father was a hardware merchant, Stewart studied architecture at Princetown University, New Jersey, where he acted while a student. By 1940 he had appeared in over twenty movies and won an Academy Award for his role in *The Philadelphia Story*. In 1941 Stewart enlisted in the Army Air Corps (he owned his own aircraft, had logged over 200 hours of civilian flying and possessed a commercial pilot's licence). In January 1942 Stewart received his commission and 'wings', and on 7 July 1942 was promoted 1st Lieutenant. Finally, in August 1943 Stewart was posted to the 445th Bomb Group (Heavy), equipped with B-24 Liberators, at Sioux City, Iowa, as Operations Officer of the 703rd Squadron. After only three weeks, on 7 July 1943, he was promoted captain and given command of the squadron on merit. In November 1943 the 445th left for Tibenham, Suffolk, England, on the Southern Ferry Route (he is pictured here, kneeling at the left, with the crew of *Tenovus* at Marrakesh, Morocco, en route), to become part of the 8th Air Force, and Stewart went with them.

Jim Kidder via Pat Ramm

The 8th Air Force already boasted one Hollywood movie star, Clark Gable, who had appeared in several movies and had won an Oscar for his role in *It Happened One Night*, made in 1934. On 12 August 1942, following the death of his wife, actress Carole Lombard (who was killed in an air crash while on a bond tour), Gable, at forty-two years of age, voluntarily enlisted as a private in the USAAF. In October 1942 he graduated from the Officers' Candidate School in Miami as a 2nd lieutenant and attended aerial gunnery school until February 1943. On the personal insistance of General Arnold, he was assigned to the 351st Bomb Group at Polebrook to make a motion picture of gunners in action. He flew a handful of combat missions, and after completing some footage for the movie *Combat America*, returned to the States in October 1943. James Stewart not only stayed longer – to the end of the war – but flew some twenty combat missions in B-24s.

via Steve Snelling

Voluptuous Varga Girl. Al Baldwin, Snuffy Smith, Mike Cameretta, Wester Cain and Tatry, ground crew of B-17F-80-BO 42-29953 *Wolfess* of the 305th Bomb Group, pose for the camera at Chelveston on 17 October 1943. *Wolfess* was lost a month later with Wetzel F. Mays' crew in a mid-air collision with 42-30666 returning from gunnery practice near Newton Bromswold on 15 November 1943. *Wolfess* rose up in front of 42-30666 and was chopped in half by the propellers. Both aircraft fell to the ground with no survivors. Varney Cline, pilot of 42-30666, had only just finished his tour of missions the day before.

USAF via Bill Donald

B-17G-5-BO 42-31134 of the 569th Bomb Squadron, 390th Bomb Group, en route to the secret German heavy water plant situated near the little Norwegian town of Rjukan, about 75 miles from Oslo, on 16 November 1943. Intelligence sources had learned that this, and the Fortresses' targets, the molybdenum mines at Knaben, and a generating plant at Vermark in the Rjukan Valley, were all connected with the German heavy water experiments which would help give the Nazis the atomic bomb. In May 1944, 42-31134 was named *Gung Ho*, and on 10 September 1944 this aircraft and Lieutenant Charles F. McIntosh's crew failed to return from a mission when it crashed at Nuremberg. Six crew were killed and three were taken prisoner.

USAF

On 18 November 1943 the Liberators in the 2nd Bomb Division received a 'frag' order for a mission to bomb the Ju 88 repair depot at Oslo-Kjeller and industrial targets in Oslo while 127 B-17s were despatched to Gelsenkirchen. Wave after wave of enemy fighters pressed home their attacks against the Liberators, and Lieutenant Rocky C. Griffith's B-24H-1-CF 41-29161 in the 67th Bomb Squadron, 44th Bomb Group, limped back across the North Sea with a badly wounded gunner, Sergeant William T. Kuban, on board, to Shipdham, where the landing gear failed to work. The flight engineer tried desperately to crank it down by hand, but this failed too. Griffith ordered seven members of the crew to bale out before he and the co-pilot, Lieutenant L.W. Grone, successfully crash-landed the badly damaged B-24 on one wheel. Two hours later repair crews checking the wreckage found two unexploded German shells in the one good engine that had brought the crew home.

Urzal P. Harvel

Three Liberators were shot down on the Oslo raid, 18 November 1943, and three more – one each from the 93rd, 392nd and 44th – were forced to land in Sweden. B-24D-30-CO 42-40128 *War Baby* flown by Lieutenant Frank Kilcheski in the 328th Bomb Squadron, 93rd Bomb Group, landed at Orebro, as did B-24H-1FO 42-7502 *Bakadori*, flown by 2nd Lieutenant Davis M. Fogerty in the 578th Bomb Squadron, 392nd Bomb Group. B-24D-15-CF 42-63971 *Helen Hywater*, the 506th Bomb Squadron, 44th Bomb Group aircraft, piloted by Captain Baxter W. Weant, circled the airfield at Trollhattan firing signal flares to inform the Swedes that they were about to land. Policy at that time called for the burning of any aircraft that landed in neutral territory, and the 44th crew set fire to their Liberator shortly after landing.

USAF

Lieutenant Frank Valesh (far left, front row) and crew of B-17G-1-BO 42-31035 *Hang the Expense* in the 100th Bomb Group, which, with tail wheel locked, careered off the runway at the start of a 'test flight' on 26 November 1943, hit two trees and demolished a barn. Fortunately, none of the three-man crew – or their two American Red Cross girl passengers – suffered serious injury. Altogether, Valesh 'lost' five *Hang The Expense* B-17s, before he completed his tour on 24 July 1944, including B-17F-20-VE 42-97560 *Hang The Expense IV*, an H2X aircraft belonging to the 96th Bomb Group, on 19 May 1944, when he crashed taking off from Thorpe Abbotts in thick fog.

USAF

Two ground crew pose in front of B-24D 42-40749 *Sack-Time Sally*, yet another example of Varga-inspired aircraft nose art, of the 389th Bomb Group. This aircraft and Lieutenant Roy E. Braly's crew failed to return on 26 November 1943, when the aircraft crashed at Drachten in Holland. Six crew died and four were made prisoners of war.

Hugh McLaren

On 26 November 1943 the 56th Fighter Group claimed no fewer than twenty-three enemy fighters shot down. This famous photo shows sixteen pilots presumed to be the victors that day. Left to right: Captain Walter V. Cook (two Bf 110s); Lieutenant Stanley Bixby 'Fats' Morrill (Bf 109); Lieutenant John P. Bryant (Bf 110); Lieutenant John H. Truluck (Fw 190); Captain Walker H. Mahurin (three Bf 110s); Lieutenant Harold E. Comstock (Bf 110); Lieutenant Colonel Dave Schilling (two Fw 190s); Major (later Colonel) Francis S. 'Gabby' Gabreski (two Bf 110s); Captain Ralph Johnson (two Bf 110s); Major James C. Stewart, Group Operations Officer (Do 217); Lieutenant Frank W. Klibbe (Bf 109); Lieutenant Jack D. Brown (Fw 190); Lieutenant Eugene O'Neil (½ Bf 110 with Lieutenant Mark K. Boyle); Lieutenant Raymond Petly (who did not score); Flight Officer Irvin E. Valenta (two Bf 110s), and Lieutenant Anthony Carcione (Me 210). Lieutenant Fred J. Christiansen, who destroyed a Bf 110, is absent from this picture, which may explain why Petly took his place in the line-up. Gabreski finished the war as the top-scoring fighter ace in Europe with twenty-eight victories. 1st Lieutenant Stanley Byron 'Fats' Morrill was killed when bombs aboard a 93rd Bomb Group Liberator, one of two which collided at Henham, near the 56th Fighter Group base at Raydon, on 29 March 1944, exploded during the brave rescue attempt to save the crew. Morrill had nine confirmed victories at the time of his death, the last on 16 March when he shot down a Fw 190 near St Dizier.

56th Fighter Group WWII Association via Alan Hague

Fortresses of the 96th Bomb Group release their bombs on the Focke Wulf factory at Bremen on 26 November 1943. Nearest aircraft is 42-6099 *Winnie C* (previously *Ruth L* of the 337th Squadron) of the 339th Bomb Squadron, which failed to return with 2nd Lieutenant Nathan L. Young's crew on 22 March 1944, when the Fortress crashed at Falkenhoehe. Six of the crew were killed, while four were made prisoners of war.

USAF

An airman contemplates spending an hour or two of his leave at the Odeon cinema in Norwich, camouflaged to help ward off the kind of bombing attacks the cathedral city had suffered during the Baedeker Blitz in 1941.

Herman Hetzel via Christine Armes

Major Birdsall and Lieutenant Colonel O'Connor smile for the camera as Colonel Fred A. Castle, 94th Bomb Group CO, congratulates Major Franklin H. 'Pappy' Colby, 410th Bomb Squadron CO, at Rougham on completion of his tour of twenty-five combat missions, 30 November 1943. At forty-one years of age, 'Pappy' was the oldest combat pilot in the 8th Air Force! Brigadier-General Castle was killed on Christmas Eve 1944 leading the 4th Wing. He was awarded a posthumous Medal of Honor.

USAF

A spread-out and vulnerable formation of B-24 Liberators of the 389th Bomb Group over a blanket of cloud en route to Ludwigshaven on 2 December 1943.

USAF

B-17G-15-DL 42-37805 of the 379th Bomb Group was assigned to the group at Kimbolton on 2 December 1943 and was christened *Carol Dawn*. It transferred to the 91st Bomb Group on 25 May 1945 and flew home on 8 June to her final resting place, at Kingman, Arizona.

Charles L. Brown

B-24D-90-CO 42-40738, *Fightin' Sam* (used as the squadron insignia), an original 389th B-24D (and at first named *The Oklahoman*), in the 566th Squadron and crew commanded by Captain Tom Conroy in his early combat days with the 'Sky Scorpions' (Conroy was killed in the Korean War). Left to right: Walt Taylor, waist gunner; Major Conroy, 566th Squadron CO; Harley Mason, co-pilot; Al Ormsby, bombardier; Harold Roodman, navigator; Robert McNair, radio operator. Kneeling: Doyle Kirkland, ball turret; Vic Scollin, waist gunner; unknown. This aircraft was lost on 5 December 1943 in a raid on Painsbosuf, France, when it was flown by Lieutenant Harvey B. Mason. Only one man from the ten-man crew survived.

The late Russ D. Hayes Collection

The 8th Air Force took over many English country houses and palatial mansions for use as command and divisional headquarters, and rest and recuperation centres ('Flak Homes'). This secluded view is of Ketteringham Hall, near Hethel, which, from December 1943 to June 1945, was used as the 2nd Bomb Division (later 2nd Air Division) Headquarters. The Hall, which dates from Tudor times, is reputed to have been the childhood home of Lady Jane Grey (1537–1554), England's shortest-reigning monarch. After the war it served as a prep school, and it was bought by Lotus Cars in 1968.

USAF

One of the additional heavy bomb groups earmarked for the 8th Air Force late in 1943 was the 458th Bomb Group, here getting ready for overseas movement at Tonopah Army Air Base, Nevada, in December 1943.

Herman Hetzel via Christine Armes

A thick pall of smoke rises from Predannack airfield, Cornwall, on 12 December 1943 from B-24H-5-FO 42-7733 *Laki-Nuki* of the 712th Bomb Squadron, 448th Bomb Group, which crash-landed after flying from Marrakesh, North Africa, during which it was hit by AA fire over France. Pilot 2nd Lieutenant Robert C. Ayrest and all fourteen aboard escaped unhurt. Ayrest was killed at Long Row, Tibenham, on 10 February 1944 while flying 42-52132 of the 712th Squadron.

via Pat Everson

B-17F-55-BO 42-29529 *Nora II* of the 364th Bomb Squadron, 305th Bomb Group, at Chelveston with 1st Lieutenant Lester Personeus' crew, who had flown 15 missions together and went on to finish with 25 missions apiece. *Nora II* transferred to the 384th Bomb Group, and 2nd Lieutenant G.J. Poole crash-landed the aircraft at Grafton Underwood on unlucky 13 December 1943.

USAF via Bill Donald

B-17G-1-BO 42-31033 *Pee Tey Kun* of the 613th Bomb Squadron, 401st Bomb Group, after crash-landing at Deenthorpe on 16 December 1943. *Pee Tey Kun* was missing in action with 1st Lieutenant Stephen J. Nasen's crew on 11 January 1944.

USAF via Mike Bailey

P-47C WW ('War Weary') Thunderbolt riding herd above a formation of 490th Bomb Group Liberators. Apart from their role as escort fighters, 'combat-fatigued' Thunderbolts were used by groups as monitor aircraft to report on formation flying, etc.

via Gordon Richards

They also served. Master Sergeant Hugh K. Crawford, crew chief of B-17F-45-BO 42-97358 *Ordnance Express* in the 94th Bomb Group at Bury St Edmunds, tends to an engine problem at Rougham in December 1944. *Ordnance Express* survived the war and finished her days at Kingman, Arizona, in November 1945, before being cut up for scrap like thousands of other Forts.

Hugh K. Crawford Collection

For some, Christmas 1943 was the Americans' second in the European Theatre of Operations. For many, like almost all of the men in this photo of 389th Bomb Group airmen at Hethel, it would be their last. For the survivors, there would be one more Christmas before final victory.

USAF

Fortresses of the 306th Bomb Group in formation early in 1944. B-17G-20-BO 42-31454 joined the Thurleigh Group on 27 December 1943 and survived to see retirement as a 'War Weary'. The B-17G version had a chin turret developed in response to the head-on attacks by the Luftwaffe.

USAF

During a ceremony on 4 January 1944, the 445th Bomb Group took possession of Tibenham from the RAF. The Group flew their first mission on 13 December 1943, and received a Distinguished Unit Citation for the 24 February 1944 raid at Gotha.

USAF

B-17F-120-BO 42-30767 in the 367th 'Clay Pigeon' Bomb Squadron, 306th Bomb Group, crashed on take-off at Thurleigh on 5 January 1944, killing the pilot, Captain Ian R. Elliott, who was flying almost his last mission, and seven of the crew.

Richards Collection

B-17F-15-VE 42-97504 *Mary Lou*, which joined the 323rd Bomb Squadron, 91st Bomb Group, on 23 January 1944. This aircraft being flown by Captain Ruxford T. Boggs was involved in a taxiing accident while on a training flight on 13 October 1944, now in the 322nd Squadron, at Kimbolton, having flown seventy missions.

via Robert E. Foose

B-17F-90-BO 42-30188 *Temptation* (formerly *Kats Sass II*) of the 413th Bomb Squadron, 96th Bomb Group, in flight. This Fortress lost an engine on take-off on 4 February 1944, and Lieutenant Joseph Meacham attempted a crash-landing at another as yet unfinished base nearby, but the aircraft crashed short, in a field at East Shropham. All of Meacham's crew walked away from the wreckage.

via Robert E. Foose

Captain David L. Wilhite's crew of B-24D-125-CO 42-41013 *Trouble 'N Mind* in the 566th Bomb Squadron, 389th Bomb Group, shown prior to being shot down over France on 7 January 1944. Back row, left to right: Sam Flatter, James McConnell, Lieutenant Harry, Captain Wilhite, Rudy Salties, Harold Saunders. Front row, left to right: Charles 'Denny' Dewett, Max Snyder, Roger Caplinger, and far right, Staff Sergeant Bob Sweatt (the only survivor that day). All the crew pictured, except the co-pilot (who was replaced by Wendell Dailey on the fateful 7 January mission) and Harry (who did not fly that day), were killed. Bob Sweatt was rescued by French Resistance workers after his parachute had been opened by the concussion of the exploding Liberator. He was unconscious when the French Underground found him, and they hid him in a secret medical facility. Later, the watch he is wearing was given to him, still running, after falling 4 miles to earth. Wilhite's crew had returned to combat duty after being released from internment in Portugal in the summer of 1943 after engine trouble prevented them from continuing to North Africa in July 1943 for the Ploesti mission.

The late Russ D. Hayes Collection

B-17F-35-VE 42-5918 *Heavenly Daze* of the 336th Bomb Squadron, 95th Bomb Group, which failed to return with Lieutenant Leslie B. Palmer's crew on 11 January 1944. One crew member was killed in action, the rest were taken prisoner.

via Steve Adams

A Messerschmitt Bf 110 attacks a formation of 91st Bomb Group B-17s approaching their target on 22 January 1944. One of the gunners described the attack thus: 'A host of enemy fighters had attacked us near the Biscay coast. They shot down seven B-17s in our group including both planes flying on our wing. The Luftwaffe really are very hot pilots and they don't scare very easy. I noticed four Me 110s at about 1,200 yards at 7 o'clock. I had my guns on them to see what they would do. They were just milling around. Then one peeled off and came into attack. I held my fire until he was about 500 yards. Then I opened up. I fired about 70 rounds. He started to burn and peeled off toward 8 o'clock. Then he threw his belly up. I let loose about 30 rounds. The pilot baled out and the plane started down and then exploded.'

USAF via Robert E. Foose

B-17G-1-BO 42-31047 *Wolverine* of the 535th Bomb Squadron, 381st Bomb Group, based at Ridgewell. An early G model, it has neither cheek guns nor Plexiglas waist window panels. *Wolverine* went missing in action with 2nd Lieutenant Robert P. Deering's crew on 30 January 1944.

USAF via Mike Bailey

In February 1944 the 56th Fighter Group at Halesworth became the first 8th Air Force fighter group to use nose colours for identification. There is, however, no mistaking the wolf insignia on Lyle Adriense's T-bolt, which of course refers to Zemke's famous 'Wolfpack'. The 56th Fighter Group opted to retain its P-47 Thunderbolts right through the war, the only fighter group to do so, and even eclipsed all the Mustang groups by destroying more enemy aircraft in combat than any other.

56th Fighter Group WWII Association via Alan Hague

Operation CROSSBOW, the all out assault on the V1 rocket sites, had begun in August 1943. 8th Air Force crews flew 'milk runs' to the 'No-Ball' sites, and to their heavily-fortified supply bunkers, in the Pas de Calais. Of the 29 missions flown by the 8th Air Force in January–February 1944, 13 were flown to V1 sites. In fact, they were anything but 'milk runs', as 1st Lieutenant James O. 'Augie' Bolin and the crew of B-24D-25-CO, Y 41-24282 *RUTH-LESS* in the 44th Bomb Group discovered on 2 February 1944, when 113 B-24s from four groups bombed a massive V1 bunker at Watten in northern France. *RUTH-LESS* had taken her name from the wife of her first pilot, Frank Slough, an ex-RCAF pilot who flew the aircraft to England on 2 February 1943 to join the 44th. *RUTH-LESS* made her combat debut on 4 April 1943, when Lieutenant Anderson flew her on a decoy mission to the Dutch coast. Slough first got to fly 'his' B-24 in the European Theatre of Operations on 1 May, another diversion mission. On 14 May *RUTH-LESS* received 125 flak holes over Kiel. In all, Slough flew seventeen missions in the aircraft, including the famous Ploesti low-level raid on 1 August 1943. The 44th was compelled to make two runs over Watten, and on the second run *RUTH-LESS* was hit by flak which damaged one engine and knocked out another, but Bolin completed the bombing run and the four 2,000 lb demolition bombs were dropped. Bolin nursed his ailing B-24 to Eastbourne, where he crashed trying to put down at an emergency landing field at Friston nearby. All the crew were killed. One crewman who had crawled from the wreckage was found two days later, when lorries and heavy lifting gear were removing the larger sections of the B-24, crushed beneath one of the Pratt & Whitney Wasp engines.

via Steve Adams

On 5 February the 3rd Bomb Division, 8th Air Force, was increased by the addition of the B-17s in the 452nd Bomb Group, commanded by Lieutenant-Colonel Herbert O. Wangeman, and based near Norwich, at Deopham Green. In these two photos, bombs from B-17s of the 452nd Bomb Group fall on the Ju88 assembly plant at Romilly, which was bombed on successive days, 5 and 6 February 1944.

Sam Young Collection

B-17F-90-BO 42-30173 *All American* (formerly *Circe*) of the 95th Bomb Group, failed to return with Lieutenant James D. Pearson's crew on 10 February 1944. Three crew were killed in action, the remaining seven were made prisoners of war.

USAF via Mike Bailey

In November 1943 the North American P-51B Mustang had entered theatre operations as a tactical fighter assigned to three groups of the tactical 9th Air Force, which on 16 October had transferred from North Africa and was reorganized in England as a tactical arm of the USAAF in the European Theatre of Operations. 8th Fighter Command had dire need for the long-range escort fighter, which could fly as far on its internal fuel as the P-47 could with drop tanks, but the first 8th Air Force unit to receive the P-51B, the 357th Fighter Group, stationed at Raydon, Essex, did not fly their first escort mission until 11 February 1944.

Merle Olmsted

B-24H-5-FO 42-7767 *C Shack Rabbit* of the 67th Bomb Squadron, 44th Bomb Group, on the mission to Oschersleben on 20 February 1944, when it was flown by 1st Lieutenant George E. Fish and crew, who were on their first mission (Fish and all his crew were killed in action two days later, on the mission to Gotha). General Jimmy Doolittle had been biding his time, waiting for a period of relatively fine weather during which to mount a series of raids on the German aircraft industry. On 20 February he sent over a force of 1,000 heavy bombers: the 1st and 2nd Bomb Divisions to the Bf 109 plants at Leipzig (bombed only a few hours earlier by RAF Bomber Command), and the 3rd Bomb Division to Posen in Poland, in the first of a series of raids during 20–25 February, which would go down in history as 'Big Week.' *Shack Rabbit* was one of eleven 44th Bomb Group B-24s lost on 8 April 1944 – the Eightballs' worst loss of the war – after being hit by fighters, on the mission to Langenhagen airfield. Lieutenant George Thom and his crew were made prisoners of war.

via Steve Adams

Bombs dropped from 19,000 ft by Liberators of the 446th Bomb Group explode near Lingen, Holland, on 21 February 1944, when many groups attacked targets of opportunity and airfields and aircraft depots because thick cloud prevented bombing the primary targets at Brunswick.

USAF

After briefing, combat crew members of the 453rd Bomb Group pile on a jeep for the trip to the flight line at Old Buckenham.

USAF

Two 453rd Bomb Group crewmen recount their mission experiences to an avid audience of British schoolchildren at Old Buckenham on 21 February 1944.

USAF

B-24H-5-DT 41-28654 *Spare Parts* of the 453rd Bomb Group en route for Old Buckenham after a raid on a Luftwaffe airfield on 21 February 1944. This aircraft finished the war and was returned to the USA at the end of the conflict.

USAF

B-17F-10-DL 42-37796 *Fletcher's Castoria II* of the 100th Bomb Group which was shot down over Holland during the mission to Brunswick on 21 February 1944 with Lieutenant William H. Fletcher's crew, who crash-landed at Halfiveg. Fletcher and all his crew were made prisoners of war.

USAF

*Overleaf:* A formation of B-24J Liberators of the 706th Bomb Squadron, 446th Bomb Group, en route to the Messerschmitt Bf 110 plant at Gotha, 420 miles due east of the white cliffs of Dover, on 22 February 1944. Intelligence described Gotha as 'the most valuable single target in the enemy twin-engine fighter complex'. B-24J-95-CO 42-100360 *Luck and Stuff*, the nearest aircraft in the formation, failed to return on 29 April 1944 with Lieutenant Weems D. Jones' crew. It crashed at Luckenwalde, Germany, killing three crew, seven being made prisoners of war.

USAF

Loading the airmail addressed to Hitler. Ground crew prepare to load 500 lb bombs aboard B-17F 42-29931 *Satan's Workshop* of the 360th Bomb Squadron, 303rd Bomb Group, for a raid on Germany. *Satan's Workshop* failed to return on 22 February 1944.

Lt Col. Harry D. Gobrecht via Brian Maguire

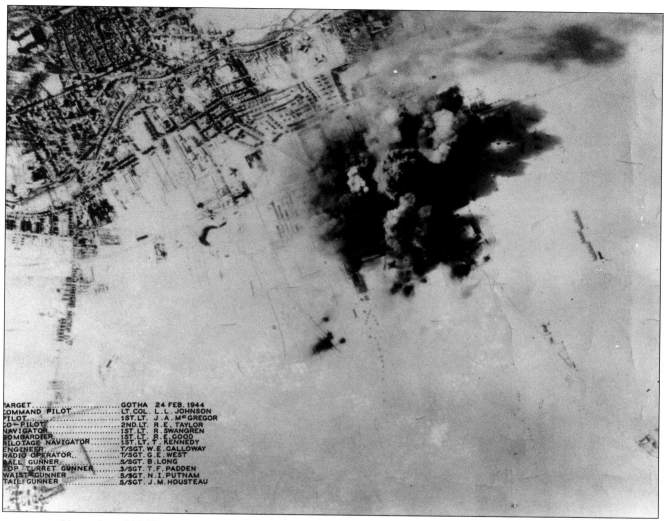

TARGET................................... GOTHA 24 FEB. 1944
COMMAND PILOT................... LT.COL. L.L.JOHNSON
PILOT..................................... 1ST.LT. J.A.McGREGOR
CO-PILOT............................... 2ND.LT. R.E.TAYLOR
NAVIGATOR............................ 1ST.LT. R.SWANGREN
BOMBARDIER.......................... 1ST.LT. R.E.GOOD
PILOTAGE NAVIGATOR........... 1ST.LT. T.KENNEDY
ENGINEER.............................. T/SGT. W.E.GALLOWAY
RADIO OPERATOR.................. T/SGT. G.E.WEST
BALL GUNNER........................ S/SGT. B.LONG
TOP TURRET GUNNER............ S/SGT. T.F.PADDEN
WAIST GUNNER...................... S/SGT. N.I.PUTNAM
TAIL GUNNER......................... S/SGT. J.M.HOUSTEAU

Altogether, 238 B-24s from eight bomb groups attacked the aircraft factories at Gotha. Flak was heavy over Lingen, and the Liberators encountered persistent attacks by the Luftwaffe. Even the arrival of three P-47 Thunderbolt groups was unable to prevent the 445th Bomb Group losing nine aircraft before the target and fifteen overall. The 392nd was extremely accurate, dropping 98 per cent of its bombs within 2,000 ft of the aiming point. The average percentage of bombs dropped by the 2nd Bomb Division which fell within 2,000 ft on visual missions under good to fair visibility in February 1944 was only 49 per cent. The 44th Bomb Group had also achieved a highly accurate bomb run. Later, it was estimated that six to seven weeks' production of Bf 110s was lost.

USAF

B-17F-15-BO 41-24490 *Jack the Ripper* of the 324th Bomb Squadron, 91st Bomb Group, went missing in action on 22 February 1944 with the loss of 1st Lieutenant James I. Considine's crew. It was the last of the original 91st Bomb Group aircraft to be lost.

USAF

Sweating them in at Horsham St Faith.

Herman Hetzel via Christine Armes

The 458th Bomb Group were fortunate to take over pre-war RAF buildings, houses and hangar facilities when they moved into Horsham St Faith in February 1944. A similar situation awaited personnel at other bases in the region, such as Bassingbourn, Duxford, Watton and Wattisham.

Herman Hetzel via Christine Armes

B-17F-105-BO 42-30434 *Betty Boop The Pistol Packin' Mama* in the 390th Bomb Group in the 3rd Bomb Division, pictured in North Africa in August 1943, crashed at Laon, France, on 25 February 1944 with the loss of Lieutenant Robert B. Bowman's crew. Two of the crew were killed in action, the rest were taken prisoner. That day marked the culmination of 'Big Week', when the USSTAF sent 1,154 bombers and 1,000 fighters to targets deep in Germany. The 3rd Bomb Division bombed the Bf 109 plant at Regensburg-Prufening in a joint raid with the Italy-based 15th Air Force. The 3rd Bomb Division met only token fighter opposition, and the bombing severely reduced output for four months. The day's raids cost the 8th Air Force thirty-one bombers. Thereafter, cloud banks over the Continent brought a premature end to 'Big Week'. Losses during 'Big Week' amounted to 226 bombers.

Gus Mencow Collection

The high losses among the heavies since October 1943 and during 'Big Week', February 1944, speeded the introduction of the B-17G, like this one (*right*) belonging to the 381st Bomb Group. More fighter groups were also assigned. On 15 October the 55th Fighter Group, equipped with the Lockheed P-38H Lightning, had entered combat, and the 20th Fighter Group, which was also equipped with the P-38H, flew its first full group mission on 28 December 1943. Bomber crews in the 8th Air Force were desperate for a long-range fighter such as the Mustang, but they would have to continue flying unescorted missions deep

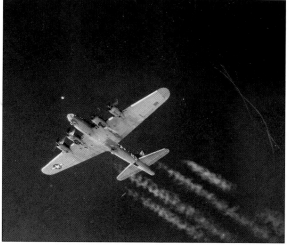

into Germany until the Mustang could be released for fighter escort missions. Meanwhile, old stagers like the P-38J had to fill the gap. These Lightnings (*below*) are from the 383rd Fighter Squadron, 364th Fighter Group, which flew their first fighter mission on 3 March 1944 from Honington, Suffolk. Nearest aircraft is 42-67978 *Betty III*.

USAF

1st Lieutenant John C. Morgan MoH ladles out soup in Stalag Luft III prisoner of war camp at Sagan in Silesia. Morgan, who won the Medal of Honor for his actions on 26 July 1943, when he left his co-pilot's seat and brought *Ruthie II* of the 92nd Bomb Group back from Hanover with a dead pilot in the cockpit, was shot down on the mission to Berlin on 6 March 1944, flying in an H2X-equipped 4th Wing lead Fortress in the 385th Bomb Group flown by Major Fred A. Rabbo and with Brigadier-General Russell Wilson on board. Their Fortress was badly hit by flak and exploded, killing eight of the crew instantly and catapulting Morgan, who was carrying a backpack parachute under his arm, out of the aircraft. He managed to put it on after several attempts, and was saved from possible injury when a tree broke his fall.

USAF

A reporter interviews Ray L. Sears (later Lieutenant-Colonel, CO of the 735th Bomb Squadron, missing in action 29 April 1944) and co-pilot Jim Kotapish from the *Reluctant Dragon* in the 453rd Bomb Group at Old Buckenham, Norfolk, on their return from Berlin on 8 March 1944. 'On this clear day there were aircraft as far ahead and as far back as the eye could see. A mass of 1,200 plus bombers and fighters that somehow made the sweating out of the bomb run a little more endurable.' The 453rd lost four B-24s on the 6 March Berlin raid, and one on 8 March.

Jim Kotapish Collection

Erkner, a suburb of Berlin, seen from 21,000 ft on 8 March 1944. The German defenders have made a spirited attempt to hinder American bombing with smoke pots. The first American bombs had fallen on 'Big B' on 4 March, when thirty-one B-17s released bombs on the Kleinmachnow area south-west of the Reich capital. Two days later the 8th despatched 730 heavies and almost 800 escort fighters to 'Big-B'; 672 bombers dropped 1,600 tons of bombs on the city, and gunners claimed over 170 German fighters destroyed, but the 8th lost 75 bombers. On 8 March 623 bombers and 891 fighters hit Berlin again. The leading Third Division lost thirty-seven Fortresses. Next day, nine more bombers were shot down by flak as the 8th tried to bomb Berlin through thick cloud. After a break in missions against the capital, on 27 March General Carl 'Toohey' Spaatz sent his bombers to Berlin again. Altogether, the 8th Air Force dropped 4,800 tons of high explosive on Berlin during five raids in March 1944.

USAF

B-17s of the 452nd Bomb Group flying at 25,000 ft above overcast en route for Berlin on 9 March 1944. The nearest aircraft is 42-39974, which failed to return with Lieutenant Ernest L. Raoener's crew on 9 April 1944. All ten men were captured and made prisoners of war.

Sam Young Collection

B-24J-65-CO 42-100073 *Sack Artists* of the 67th Bomb Squadron, 44th Bomb Group, which crash-landed at Fehraltdorf, Switzerland, during the mission to the Manzell Air Armaments factory at Freidrichshafen on 18 March 1944. 1st Lieutenant Raymond J. Lacombe and crew were interned. Five more 44th Bomb Group B-24s also landed in Switzerland on this day.

via Steve Adams

Hitting the sack. An exhausted airman is caught napping, literally, after a long, tiring mission over Germany.

Herman Hetzel via Christine Armes

Newly arrived and modified B-24s on the hangar line at Base Air Depot No. 2, Warton, Lancashire, on 10 March 1944. (Burtonwood was designated Base Air Depot No. 1, and Langford Lodge in Northern Ireland was designated Base Air Depot No. 3.) The repair plant at Burtonwood, near Liverpool, was probably the largest military base in Europe during the Second World War, processing over 11,500 aircraft between 1943 and 1945 alone, but beyond that it was responsible for the support of the 8th, 9th, 12th and 15th Air Forces. Over 35,000 men were under the direct control of Burtonwood, with 18,500 on the base itself.

*via Robert E. Foose*

B-24-1-FO 42-7507 *Heaven Can Wait* of the 68th Bomb Squadron, 44th Bomb Group, had previously served with the 392nd Bomb Group at Wendling, Norfolk. On 12 March 1944, returning from Siracourt, France, Lieutenant Sam H. Bowman III crash-landed this aircraft (for the second time in a few weeks), out of fuel, at Friston, Sussex. She was later salvaged. Bowman completed his tour on 11 July 1944.

*via Steve Adams*

A B-17 of the 452nd Bomb Group about to release its bombs over Augsburg on 16 March 1944.

Sam Young Collection

B-17s of the 452nd Bomb Group en route to Bordeaux on 27 March 1944.

Sam Young Collection

P-51B *Suga* of the 355th Fighter Group at Steeple Morden, Cambridgeshire. The white cowl band and spinner began to appear on the Group's Mustangs in late March 1944.

USAF

1st Lieutenant (later Captain) Huie Lamb of the 78th Fighter Group poses in front of his P-47 Thunderbolt at Duxford. The distinctive black-and-white checkerboard squares applied to the engine cowling shutters were introduced during the first week of April 1944.

via Andy Height

A scattered trail of propaganda leaflets leads to B-17-15-VE 42-97469 *Busy Baby* of the 527th Bomb Squadron, 379th Bomb Group, at dispersal at Kimbolton on 8 April 1944. This aircraft was declared war-weary in January 1945.

USAF via Mike Bailey

B-24D-160-CO 42-72858 *Pistol Packin' Mama* lifts off from Shipdham. On 9 April 1944 Lieutenant Hiram C. Palmer was forced to land *Pistol Packin' Mama* at Bulltofta, Sweden, after sustaining damage on the Berlin-Marienburg mission, and all ten crew were interned. The Eightballs' assembly aircraft, B-24D-1-CO 41-23699 *Lemon Drop*, a veteran of the Ploesti mission of 1 August 1943, can be seen in front of the hangar.

Bill Robertie

B-17G-45-BO 42-97212 of the 339th Bomb Squadron, 96th Bomb Group, piloted by 1st Lieutenant Sherman Gillespie, seeks refuge at Malmö, Sweden, shadowed by a Swedish Air Force J9 fighter after being damaged by enemy fighters on the mission to Rostock on 11 April 1944. In all, nine B-17s landed in Sweden on this day, and Gillespie's was one of eleven lost to the 96th. One was shot down by a Luftwaffe intruder over Suffolk.

USAF

174

Sunday morning after the Saturday night before – some party! On 22 April 1944 the Liberators of the 2nd Bomb Division were sent off late in the day to bomb the marshalling yards at Hamm, Germany. Their return, in darkness, was shadowed by Me 410s of KG51, which succeeded in shooting down several B-24s in their circuits in Norfolk and Suffolk and generally caused mayhem over the bases. One of the worst-hit was the 448th Bomb Group base at Seething, where five Liberators crashed at the end of the runway. In this photo, B-24H-1-DT 41-28595 *Ice Cold Katie* lies between B-24H-5-CF 41-29240 *Tondelayo*, flown by Lieutenant J.L. Barak, and, on the right, B-24H-15-CF 41-9575, *The Ruth E K Allah Hassid*. In all, thirteen Liberators crashed or crash-landed in east Norfolk on the night of 22 April. Two more were damaged on the ground. Over sixty men were killed, and another twenty-three injured. The fires at Seething were not extinguished until 03.30 the following morning.

via Francis X. Sheehan

*Opposite*: 453rd Bomb Group crew members inspect the damage to their B-24 at Old Buckenham on 20 April 1944 after suffering a direct flak hit in the rear of the aircraft which killed the tail gunner on the mission to Wizernes in the Pas-de-Calais. Left to right: Staff Sergeant Bruce P. Prosser, gunner; 1st Lieutenant James S. Munsey, flying with the new crew on its first combat mission; Staff Sergeant Walter J. Thomas, waist gunner. Munsey and four of his crew were killed two days later, when B-24H-10-FO 42-52186 *Cee Gee II*, named after his daughter Carol Geane, was shot down by Leutnant Nommining of II./KG51 in an Me 410 15 miles off the East Coast while returning from Hamm, Germany. Munsey was posthumously awarded the Distinguished Service Cross, which was later presented to his 2½-year-old daughter.

USAF

Flying Fw 190A-7 *Red 23*, Major Heinz 'Pritzl' Bär (centre), *Kommandeur* of II./JG1, recorded his 200th victory of the war on 22 April when he shot down B-24H-10-CF 41-29273 *Flak Magnet* of the 753rd Bomb Squadron, 458th BG. Lieutenant George N. Spaven, the pilot, was killed, but the rest of the crew survived and were made prisoners of war. Bär, who scored his first victory of the war on 25 September 1939 when he shot down a French Curtis Hawk 75, shot down at least 21 'dicke Autos' ('Fat Cars' as the American heavy bombers were called by the Luftwaffe), and his 220 victories place him eighth in the list of *Experten*. Of these, 124 were British, French and American types – more than any other German pilot except Hans-Joachim Marseille, who achieved all his victories (151) in North Africa. Oberst-leutnant (Lieutenant Colonel) Bär commanded the jet fighter school at Lechfeld from January 1945, where he flew the He 162A-2 Volksjäger, and finally *Jagdverband* 44 (scoring 16 victories on the Me 262). The Luftwaffe *experte* led a charmed life during the war – he baled out four times and was forced down on 14 occasions, only to die in a light aircraft accident in 1957.

via Eric Mombeek

Mary Ruffner, née Speight, a Land Army girl, became yet another 'GI bride' when she married Doc Anderson of 8th AAF Service Command from Milton Ernest, Bedfordshire, at the village church on 25 April 1944, complete with Land Army Girl 'honour guard'. Some 70,000 British girls married American servicemen during the Second World War.

Richards Collection

On 28 April 1944 the 100th Bomb Group was assigned a 'No-Ball' (V1) site at Sottevast, near Cherbourg. It was led by Colonel Robert H. Kelly, freshly arrived from the States just nine days before. Flak was heavy, the bomb run was abandoned, and the B-17s went around again in what one crew member described as 'the longest 360 in recorded history'. Kelly's Fortress was hit, and disentegrated without exploding, and another B-17 was also lost. Every other Fortress received hits and damage. Staff Sergeant John Bernard Palmquist (pictured), the ball turret gunner on Lieutenant Ralph W. Wright's crew, was hit, a piece of shrapnel going through his shoulder. This was the only time that the cherubic young gunner could actually 'smell' flak. Palmquist was hospitalized, and was still bedridden on 7 May when the 'Bloody Hundredth' went to Berlin. Just as they were leaving England, Wright's B-17G- 25-DL 42-38053 dived out of formation on fire. Flares, carried in the top turret compartment, had exploded. The Fortress crashed into a wooded area at Herringfleet Hall near Lowestoft, where it exploded, killing both pilots, the navigator, bombardier and replacement waist gunner.

John A. Miller Collection

In this delightful H.E. Bates photo, a Gypsy caravan owned by the Smith family, who overwintered in Yeldon, passes along a back road at Chelveston adjoining a revetment where B-17-115-BO 42-30704 *Dinah Mite* of the 364th Bomb Squadron, 305th Bomb Group, is parked. *Dinah Mite* was used for the first Monroe leaflet bomb experiments, and was written off on 15 May following a night-fighter attack. Dave Bremmer, the ball turret gunner, was killed in action.

via Bill Donald

The story of a tragic double error is told by these stomach-jolting photographs of a stick of 1,000 lb bombs dropped from Lieutenant John Winslett's B-17 *Trudy*, of the 332nd Bomb Squadron, 94th Bomb Group, over Berlin on 19 May 1944. One of the bombs knocked off the left horizontal stabilizer of Lieutenant Marion Ulysses Reid's B-17G-20-BO 42-31540 *Miss Donna Mae* of the 331st Bomb Squadron below. Reid's aircraft went into an uncontrollable spin, and at 13,000 ft the wing broke off, and the B-17 spun crazily to the ground. There were no survivors.

USAF via Abe Dolim

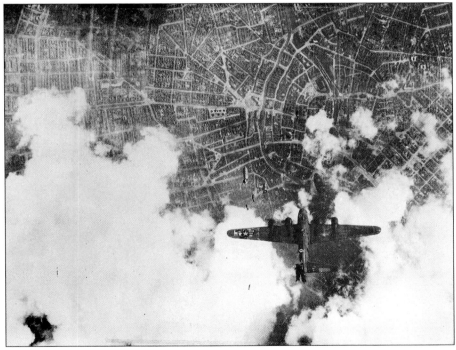

B-24H-15-FO 42-52693 *Aries* of the 834th 'Zodiacs' Bomb Squadron, 486th Bomb Group, over Lutzkendorf on 28 May 1944. This aircraft was one of several squadron aircraft re-assigned to the 801st Carpetbagger Group when the Third Division began converting to the Fortress in the summer of 1944.

USAF

B-24H-20-FO 42-94796Q of the 391st Bomb Squadron, 34th Bomb Group, *Me Worry?*, flown by 2nd Lieutenant James F. Adams, at Bulltofta, Sweden, after landing at the neutral country's airfield on 29 May 1944.

via Mike Bailey

The 3rd Strategic Air Depot at Watton-Griston, Norfolk, carried out thousands of repairs on Second Bomb Division B-24s. The most unusual must have been to B-24H-20-CF 42-50328 of the 506th Bomb Squadron, 44th Bomb Group, which Lieutenant Conrad 'Connie' Menzel successfully crash-landed in a field near Shipdham on 29 May 1944, returning from a mission to Politz. The left landing gear collapsed and the aircraft was extensively damaged. The temporary installation of a telegraph pole in the bomb bay enabled the Liberator to be flown out of the field on 10 June by a recovery crew to Watton for repairs. Upon return to duty the B-24 was affectionately referred to as 'Pregnant Peg' or the 'Flying Log'. On 8 August 1944 she crashed and exploded with a full load of bombs near Shipdham after losing an engine and aborting the mission to Le Perthe, France, shortly after take-off. 2nd Lieutenant Myron G. Jacobs and his crew were killed.

USAF

B-17G-35-BO 42-32076 *Shoo Shoo Baby* of the 401st Bomb Squadron, 91st Bomb Group, was named by its crew after a popular song of the day. On 29 May 1944 it took Lieutenant Paul McDuffee's crew to Frankfurt on the first of twenty-four combat missions in which it was damaged by flak on seven occasions. Her last mission was to Posnan, Poland, on 29 May 1944, when engine problems forced Lieutenant Robert Guenther's crew to make a landing in neutral Sweden. The Swedish government was officially given seven B-17s as a gift, and in exchange American crews were repatriated. *Shoo Shoo Baby's* nose was lengthened by 3 ft and accommodation provided for fourteen passengers and 4,400 lb of cargo in the bomb bay. In 1955, after Swedish and Danish airline service and Danish military use, the aircraft was bought by a New York company and sold to the Institute Géographique National in Paris. In July 1978 *Shoo Shoo Baby* was flown by C-5 Galaxy to Dover Air Force Base, Delaware, and after a ten-year restoration to flying condition, was flown to the USAF Museum at Wright-Patterson Air Force Base, Dayton, Ohio, on 13 October 1988, where *Shoo Shoo Baby* is now on permanent display.

via Frank Thomas

# INDEX